PRACTICAL GOURMET

Company's Coming ®

Campfire Cooking

Morrison • Paré • Darcy

Library and Archives Canada Cataloguing in Publication

Morrison, Jeff, 1967-, author
    Campfire cooking / Jeff Morrison, Jean Paré, James Darcy.

(Practical Gourmet Company's Coming)
Includes index.
ISBN 978-1-988133-38-6 (softcover)

    1. Outdoor cooking. 2. Cookbooks. I. Paré, Jean, 1927-, author II. Darcy, James, author III. Title. IV. Series: Practical Gourmet Company's Coming

TX823.M665 2017   641.5'78   C2017-900709-2

Cover credits: *Front cover:* Sandy Weatherall. *Back cover:* Sandy Weatherall

All inside photos are by Sandy Weatherall except: p. 1 (Bondariev), p. 3 (pavel_klimenko). p. 4 (Bruskov), p. 6 (EJJohnsonPhotography), p. 7 (welcomia), p. 8 (seksanwangjaisuk), p. 8 (catalin_grigoriu), p. 9 (vovik_mar), p. 11 (wellphoto), p. 13 (SarapulSar38), p. 15 (lamthatiam), p. 17 (ersler), p. 19 (loooby), p. 21 (BSANI), p. 23 (al62), p. 25 (voltan1), p. 27 (StasyaLee), p. 29 (BaronVisi), p. 35 (HandmadePictures), p. 37 (martinturzak), p. 39 (treasurephoto), p. 41 (coffemug), p. 44 (Wildnerdpix), p. 45 (seread), p. 46-47 (FrankieCarr), p 51 (Digoarpi), p. 52-53 (ongap), p. 57 (martiapunts), p. 59 (AnjelaGr), p. 61 (DGerriePhotography), p. 64 (itsajoop), p. 65 (Vegfrt), p. 67 (voltan1), p. 71 (bhofack2), p. 77 (Scukrov), p. 80 (Vitalalp), p. 81 (Svetlanka777), p. 83 (bhofack2), p. 85 (Pronina_Marina), p. 87 (joyt), p. 89 (JoaBal), p. 93 (CharlieAJA), p. 95 (Ivenks), p. 96 (ralphradford), p. 97(JZHunt), p. 97 (conceptphotos), p. 105 (cookedphotos), p. 107 (Sapunovaphoto), p. 109 (SonjaBK), p. 117 (bhofack2), p. 118 (Hemera Technologies), p. 119 (tolstnev), p. 121 (gontabunta), p. 125 (AlexPro9500), p 131 (nicolesy), p. 135 (alblec), p. 137 (Monkey Business Images), p. 140 (artoleshko), p. 141 (Sitikka), p. 142-143 (BANNOCK PHOTO). p 145 (styxclick), p. 147 (EJJohnsonPhotography), p. 149 (cobraphoto), p. 151 (Lisovskaya), p. 152-153 (MSPhotographic), courtesy Thinkstock.

Distributed by
Canada Book Distributors - Booklogic
11414-119 Street
Edmonton. Alberta, Canada T5G 2X6
Tel: 1-800-661-9017

We acknowledge the financial support of the Government of Canada.

Funded by the Government of Canada
Financé par le gouvernement du Canada | Canadä

PC: 28

Table of Contents

Practical Gourmet

Good company and great food are a powerful combination. When laughter and conversation mix with the heady fragrance and flavours of delicious fare, we are not just sharing a meal—we are nourishing our lives. Artfully prepared dishes awaken the senses and please the palate. And here's the secret: It can be so simple!

Practical Gourmet is delighted to partner with **Company's Coming** to introduce a new series designed to help home cooks create no-fuss, sumptuous food. It is possible to wow both the eye and the palate using readily available ingredients and minimal effort. Practical Gourmet offers recipes without the hassle of complicated methods, special equipment or obscure ingredients.

Titles in this series feature step-by-step instructions, full-page colour photos with every recipe, menu suggestions and sidebars on preparation tips and tricks.

Approachable recipe, fabulous results, wonderful get-togethers—it all starts with *Campfire Cooking!*

The Jean Paré Story

Jean Paré (pronounced "jeen PAIR-ee") grew up understanding that the combination of family, friends and home cooking is the best recipe for a good life. When Jean left home, she took with her a love of cooking, many family recipes and an intriguing desire to read cookbooks as if they were novels!

When her four children had all reached school age, Jean volunteered to cater the 50th anniversary celebration of the Vermilion School of Agriculture, now Lakeland College, in Alberta, Canada. Working from her home, Jean prepared a dinner for more than 1,000 people and from there launched a flourishing catering operation that continued for more than 18 years.

As requests for her recipes increased, Jean was often asked, "Why don't you write a cookbook?" The release of *150 Delicious Squares* on April 14, 1981, marked the debut of what would soon turn into one of the world's most popular cookbook series.

"Never share a recipe you wouldn't use yourself."

Company's Coming cookbooks are distributed in Canada, the United States, Australia and other world markets. Bestsellers many times over in English, Company's Coming cookbooks have also been published in French and Spanish.

Familiar and trusted in home kitchens around the world, Company's Coming cookbooks are offered in a variety of formats. Highly regarded as kitchen workbooks, the softcover Original Series, with its lay-flat plastic comb binding, is still a favourite among home cooks.

Jean Paré's approach to cooking has always called for quick and easy recipes using everyday ingredients. That view served her well, and the tradition continues in the Practical Gourmet series.

Jean's Golden Rule of Cooking is: Never share a recipe you wouldn't use yourself. It's an approach that has worked—millions of times over!

Introduction

Camping, hiking and just spending time outdoors are activities enjoyed by a vast number of people in Canada and the United States. Statistics show that North Americans spend almost 20 percent more nights in an average year at campgrounds than in hotels and motels. Yes, it is true; we do enjoy getting back to nature.

Outdoor enthusiasts live for the brief moments in which they can trade the frantic pace of the city for the sight of a meteor shower at night or the echo of a coyote's howl over the ridge; when they can swap the hustle and bustle of daily life for the peace and tranquility of nature. Whether you are trekking hundreds of kilometres into the backwoods or heading to the provincial park just an hour from your house, getting back to nature is the ultimate form of rejuvenation.

When getting out of town to experience what Mother Nature has to offer, we have varying preferences. Some like to rough it in a tent or even construct their own primitive lean-to or shelter, whereas others prefer the comfort and convenience of a chalet, cottage or trailer. The type of accommodations you choose doesn't really matter; the key component of any successful wilderness outing is the campfire.

The warming glow of a campfire has served as the focal point for some of my favourite gatherings of family and friends. There is something alluring and downright sexy about a campfire. It is like the gift that keeps on giving and is said to "warm you twice," once by the physical activity of cutting, splitting and piling the firewood and again, later on, when the wood is burned.

Yes, a good campfire can attract visitors from far and wide, who will be quick to gather and stare contently into the flames as if they were some rare and miraculous occurrence sent from the heavens. A campfire, when properly constructed, can be an excellent source of heat, and when the wood burns down on your fire lay, that glowing bed of coals serves as the perfect heat source for cooking. That special blend of paper, kindling, hardwood fire logs, oxygen and flames come together to form the mainstay of any outdoor adventure.

The one aspect that none of us hope to scrimp on when outdoors is the food we eat. As our interest in spending time camping and sleeping in the outdoors increases, so too does our ability to whip up a well-thought-out meal, cooked on the open fire. There is a sense of accomplishment with putting together a tasty meal without the modern convenience of electricity. You would not believe the wonderful meals that can be cooked over a campfire.

Campfire Cooking emphasizes meals that are easily and efficiently prepared over the common campfire lay. Even when roughing it in the great outdoors, one does not need to starve or settle for substandard fare. As you will see in these pages, there are many options for crafting tasty and nutritious meals right over the open fire. From appetizers and mains to sides and even sweet, delicious desserts, all aspects of the perfectly balanced meal come to fruition right before your eyes on the campfire. We are not just talking hot dogs and marshmallows cooked on sticks over the flames (though they are also delicious); we are talking such classic comfort foods as shepherd's pie, mac and cheese, nachos and bread pudding. Once your fire has burned down past the open flame stage, the glowing embers that remain continue to offer heat for an assortment of the most perfect meals you can envision.

After spending more than four decades exploring the wondrous North American wilderness, I've amassed a vast repertoire of tips and tricks for campfire cooking, which I present to you in this book, along with preparation hints on planning (and executing) a variety of awesome recipes completed from start to finish over an open fire.

So pull up a comfy camping chair and prime your taste buds for a selection of my campfire favourites. I look forward to sharing a sampling of culinary gems that will make your next adventure afield more fulfilling, and heck of a lot tastier!

Beef Ragout

When planning for more lengthy adventures afield, deciding what proteins to cook can often be a daunting task. I usually try to round things out by serving at least one meal each of chicken, pork, lamb, fish and beef. This beef ragout recipe covers the beef night in an effective and satisfying way.

Chopped onion	2 cups	500 mL
Garlic cloves, minced	2	2
Butter	2 tbsp.	30 mL
Boneless inside round (or blade or chuck) steak, trimmed of fat and cubed	2 lbs.	900 g
Reserved tomato juice, plus water to make	1 cup	250 mL
Bay leaves	2	2
Pepper	1/4 tsp.	1 mL
Whole baby carrots	2 cups	500 mL
Whole small fresh mushrooms	2 cups	500 mL
Can of stewed tomatoes (14 oz., 398 mL), drained and juice reserved	1	1
Medium green pepper, slivered	1	1
Paprika	2 tsp.	10 mL
Seasoned salt	1 tsp.	5 mL
Water	1/3 cup	75 mL
All-purpose flour	2 tbsp.	30 mL

Sauté onion and garlic in butter in a large frying pan over medium until onion is soft and golden. Transfer to a ungreased 3 quart (3 L) casserole and add next 4 ingredients. Cook, covered, in 325°F (160°C) oven for 1 1/2 hours.

Stir in next 6 ingredients. Cook, covered, for about 1 hour until beef is tender. Remove and discard bay leaves.

Stir water into flour in a small cup until smooth. Stir into beef mixture and cook, covered, for 15 minutes until bubbling and thickened. Allow to cool before transporting. When ready to serve, heat in a large pot or Dutch oven directly on your heat source at campground. Makes 10 cups (2.5 L).

Chipotle Burgers

These burgers add just the right amount of kick and smoky flavour, making them an ideal choice to enjoy around the fire. Gone are the days of those bland, dry burgers your parents served while camping when you were a child. These burgers offer just the right amount of heat and are super juicy when cooked outdoors over the open campfire.

Mayonnaise	1/3 cup	75 mL
Finely chopped chipotle peppers in adobo sauce	1 tsp.	5 mL
Grated orange zest	1/2 tsp.	5mL
Finely chopped red onion	2 tbsp.	30 mL
Crushed seasoned croutons	2 tbsp.	30 mL
Finely chopped chipotle peppers in adobo sauce	1 tsp.	5 mL
Salt	1/4 tsp.	1 mL
Lean ground beef	1 lb.	454 g
Hamburger buns, split	4	4
Lettuce leaves	4	4
Medium avocado, sliced	1	1
Medium tomato slices	4	4
Medium red onion slices (optional)	4	4
Bacon slices, cooked crisp, cut in half	4	4
Finely shredded fresh basil (optional)	1/4 cup	60 mL

Combine first 3 ingredients in a small bowl.

Combine next 4 ingredients in a large bowl. Add beef and mix well. Form mixture into 1 inch (2.5 cm) thick patties. Refigerate until ready to cook.

To cook, place on a grid about 2 inches (5 mL) above open coals. Flip regularly and cook until slightly pink in centre. Serve with remaining 7 ingredients. Makes 4 burgers.

Reflector Oven Shepherd's Pie

Prepare the recipe at home and finish it in your reflector oven at your campsite. With everything prepared in advance, dinner will require no on-site preparation except that you will need to build a good fire and place your reflector oven in the ideal location.

Russet potatoes	1 1/2 lbs.	680 g
Vegetable oil	2 tbsp.	30 mL
Onion, chopped	1	1
Carrots, peeled and diced	2	2
Minced garlic	2 tsp.	10 mL
Ground lamb	1 1/2 cups	375 mL
Salt	1 tsp.	5 mL
Pepper	1/2 tsp.	2 mL
All purpose flour	2 tbsp.	30 mL
Tomato paste	2 tsp.	10 mL
Chicken broth	1 cup	250 mL
Worcestershire sauce	1 tsp.	5 mL
Chopped rosemary	2 tsp.	10 mL
Chopped thyme leaves	1 tsp.	5 mL
Butter	2 tbsp.	30 mL
Milk	1/4 cup	60 mL
Salt	3/4 tsp.	4 mL
Pepper	1/4 tsp.	1 mL
Egg yolk	1	1
Kernel corn	1/2 cup	125 mL
Green peas	1/2 cup	125 mL

Peel potatoes and cut into 1/2-inch (12 mm) pieces. Place in a medium saucepan and cover with cold water. Bring to a boil over high heat. Reduce heat and simmer, covered, until potatoes are tender, about 10 to 15 minutes.

Heat oil in a 12 inch (30 cm) sauté pan over medium high. Add onion and carrots and sauté for 3 or 4 minutes. Stir in garlic.

Add lamb and first amount of salt and pepper, and cook until lamb is browned and cooked through, about 3 minutes. Sprinkle meat with flour and toss to coat. Cook for 1 to 2 minutes.

Add next 5 ingredients and stir to combine. Bring to a boil, and then reduce heat to low and simmer, covered, for 10 to 12 minutes until sauce is thickened slightly.

Drain potatoes. Add butter and allow it to melt. Mash potatoes and add milk and second amount of salt and pepper. Continue to mash until smooth. Stir in yolk until well combined.

Transfer meat mixture to a medium Dutch oven. Stir in corn and peas. Spread mashed potatoes over top using a rubber spatula. Keep shepherd's pie cool in refrigerator or cooler until ready to use.

To cook, place shepherd's pie in your reflector oven as you would in a normal oven and heat until centre is hot and sauce is bubbling. Makes 5 servings.

Campfires can be built with natural reflectors by sitting the fire beside a rock face. The rocks will heat up and bounce the heat back towards the fire. Food can be placed between the fire and the rock to take advantage of the heat.

Teriyaki Steak

This Asian twist on grilled campfire steak will please even the finickiest eater. When choosing a suitable rib-eye cut of beef for this recipe, look for pieces with a nice balance of meat and marbling. Leaner cuts of beef can be more difficult to cook over the fire because they tend to dry out quickly when grilling.

Soy sauce	1/4 cup	60 mL
Cooking sherry	2 tbsp.	30 mL
Granulated sugar	1 tbsp.	15 mL
Garlic clove, minced	1	1
Freshly grated ginger root	1/2 tsp.	2 mL
Pepper	1/4 tsp.	1 mL
Rib-eye (or sirloin) steak, 1 inch (2.5 cm) thick	1 1/2 lbs.	680 g

Combine first 6 ingredients in a small saucepan. Heat, stirring, until sugar is dissolved. Set aside to cool. Once cool, transfer to a sealable container for transporting.

At your campsite, brush both sides of steak with sauce. Prepare a hot bed of coals and lay your cooking grid 1 to 2 inches (2.5 to 5 cm) above coals. Cook steaks for about 10 minutes per side, flipping no more than twice until steak is firm to touch but still light pink in centre. Makes 4 servings.

૭ If stored properly, ginger root can last up to 6 months. Just wrap the unpeeled root tightly in plastic and freeze. When you are preparing a recipe that calls for ginger root, cut off the quantity you are going to use and put the rest back in the freezer.

Caribbean Brochettes

Soaking wood skewers is something many people forget to do, but it is an important task, especially when cooking on an outdoor heat source. Most experts suggest soaking skewers for at least 30 minutes but no more than 2 hours because they become too soft. For those who find soaking skewers too tedious, opt for metal skewers instead. I have found that square- or triangular-shaped skewers work much better than the traditional rounded ones—they hold the meat and vegetables more securely so that food doesn't spin around as you turn the skewers in the grill.

Pineapple juice	1 cup	250 mL
Finely grated lime zestl (about 1 medium)	1 tbsp.	15 mL
Freshly squeezed lime juice (about 1 medium)	1/4 cup	60 mL
Small onion, finely chopped	1	1
Finely chopped ginger root	1 tsp.	5 mL
Hot pepper sauce	1/4 tsp.	1 mL
Beef sirloin, cut into 1 inch (2.5 cm) cubes	1 1/2 lbs.	680 g

Combine first 6 ingredients in a small sealable container for transporting.

At the campsite, add beef to container and let marinate in a cooler or refrigerator for 4 hours. If using wooden skewers, soak in water for 30 minutes. Prepare campfire. Remove beef from marinade and discard remaining marinade. Thread meat cubes onto skewers and cook for about 8 minutes, until beef is slightly pink and hot in centre. Makes 5 servings.

When a recipe calls for grated zest and juice, it's easier to grate the fruit first, and then juice it. Be careful not to grate down to the pith (white part of the peel), which is bitter and best avoided.

Hearty Hamburger Vegetable Soup

Let's face it, it would be great if every day of camping was sunny and warm, but unfortunately there will be cold and rainy days. This is the perfect make ahead lunch or dinner for those not-so-nice-weather camping days.

Ground beef	1 1/2 lbs.	680 g
Onion, chopped	1	1
Green pepper, chopped	1	1
Carrots, chopped	3	3
Celery ribs, chopped	3	3
Barley	1/2 cup	125 mL
Can of diced tomatoes (28 oz., 796 mL)	1	1
Water	2 cups	500 mL
Beef broth	3 cups	750 mL
Can of condensed tomato soup (10 oz., 284 mL)	1	1
Bay leaf	1	1
Parsley	1 tbsp.	15 mL
Garlic clove, minced	1	1
Dried thyme	1/2 tsp.	2 mL
Pepper, to taste		

Heat a large cast iron pot or Dutch oven on medium-high heat. Crumble in ground beef and cook until the beef is evenly browned. Drain grease.

Stir in next 5 ingredients.

Add remaining 9 ingredients and bring to a boil. Reduce heat and simmer, covered, for 1 1/2 to 2 hours, stirring frequently. Allow to cool before transporting. Wrap plastic wrap on top of pot between the lid and pot. When ready to serve, remove plastic wrap and place pot directly on your heat source at campground until soup is heated through. Remove bay leaf before serving. Makes 6 servings.

Homemade Pasta Sauce

Any way you look at it, this homemade pasta sauce has the taste and feel of home written all over it. One of my favourite comfort foods while spending time in the great outdoors, this hearty dish. It makes for a perfect larger lunch or dinner meal and will have dinner guests coming back for more.

Butter	1/2 cup	125 mL
Olive oil	3 tbsp.	45 mL
Large onion, diced	1	1
Garlic cloves, minced	3	3
Ground beef	1 lb.	454 g
Ground sausage	1 lb.	454 g
Italian seasoning	4 tsp.	20 mL
Salt	2 tsp.	10 mL
Pepper	1/2 tsp.	2 mL
Dried oregano	1 1/2 tsp.	5 mL
Water	9 1/2 cups	2.4 L
Cans of tomato paste (6 oz., 170 mL, each)	3	3
Can of tomato sauce (29 oz., 860 mL)	1	1

Heat butter, oil, onion and garlic in a large pot over medium. Add ground beef and sausage and cook until browned and crumbly.

Add Italian seasoning, salt, pepper and oregano and simmer for 20 minutes.

Add water, tomato paste and tomato sauce. Simmer, stirring occasionally, for at least 2 hours. This sauce can be frozen for easier transport. You might want to freeze it in batches as this recipe makes too much for one meal. Once you are at your camping destination, simply heat the sauce in a pot over your fire. Makes 30 servings.

When cooking spaghetti, consider using a frying pan. Simply lie the pasta flat, add enough cold water to cover it and put it on the heat to boil. It will cook just fine, with no need for cups and cups of water, especially when you are camping and may have a limited supply of water and few choices of cookware.

Best Ever Ribs

This old family favourite will have the meat falling off the bone and you and your dinner guests falling out of your chairs when you eat it.

Clam tomato beverage	**2 cups**	**500 mL**
Water	**1 cup**	**250 mL**
Pork back ribs	**4 lbs.**	**1.8 kg**
Bottled barbecue sauce	**2 cups**	**500 mL**

Add clam tomato beverage and water to cover bottom of a large roasting pan with lid. Place ribs on a rack inside roasting pan so that they are not sitting in juices. Cook, covered, in a 250°F (120°C) oven for 3 hours. Remove ribs from oven and set aside to cool (or meat will fall off the bone and it will be hard to remove from roasting pan). Transfer to a large resealable freezer bag or container for transport.

To cook, brush ribs with barbecue sauce and place on a grid set about 2 inches (5 mL) above open coals. Cook for 5 minutes per side. Remove from grid and serve. Makes 4 servings.

I love the culture of grilling. It creates an atmosphere that is festive but casual.
—Bobby Flay

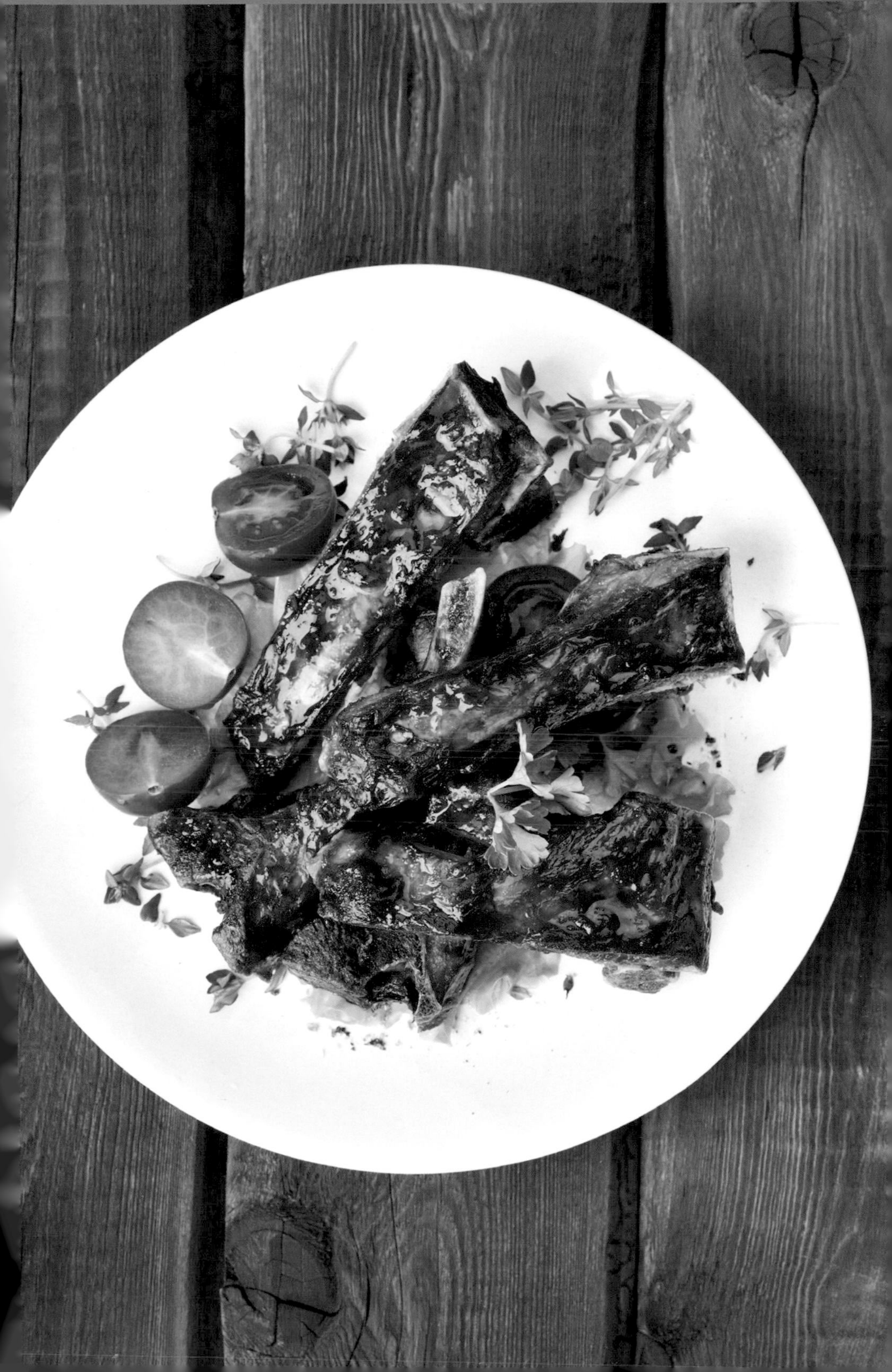

Smoked Pork Steaks

In this recipe, you will be doing most of the work at home, which is making the dry rub. You could double, or even triple, the dry rub recipe and keep it in your camping pack for future trips.

Kosher salt	2 tbsp.	30 mL
Pepper	2 tbsp.	30 mL
Granulated sugar	2 tbsp.	30 mL
Garlic powder	3 tbsp.	45 mL
Onion powder	2 tbsp.	30 mL
Paprika	3 tbsp.	45 mL
Ground sage	1 tbsp.	15 mL
Dried oregano	2 tsp.	10 mL
Dry mustard	1 tsp.	5 mL
Cayenne pepper	1 tsp.	5 mL
Pork steaks, 2 inches (5 cm) thick	**2**	**2**

Combine first 10 ingredients to create your dry rub. Store it in a small resealable freezer bag or spice container.

To prepare steaks, rub dry rub on pork steaks, wrap in plastic wrap and set in a cooler or refrigerator for at least 8 hours to marinate. To cook, remove steaks from plastic wrap and place on a grill over indirect coals. Cook slowly, turning pork occasionally, until it is tender and reaches an internal temperature of 185°F (85°C), about 2 hours. Serve with your favourite barbecue sauce or as is. Makes 2 servings.

Grilled Pork Tenderloin

A true family favourite, this grilled pork tenderloin is just about the most delectable protein one can cook over the campfire. Because the tenderloin cut is inherently free of fat, cooking it on the grill requires an attentive eye. It can burn very easily and must be turned constantly for the best and most consistent cook throughout. Be sure to let the meat stand for 2 to 3 minutes after cooking, and then cut it into 3/4 inch (2 cm) slices for serving.

Soy sauce	1 cup	250 mL
Granulated sugar	6 tbsp	90 mL
Small onion, minced	1/2	1/2
Minced garlic	4 tsp.	20 mL
Finely chopped ginger root	2 tsp.	10 mL
Vegetable oil	1/4 cup	60 mL
Pork tenderloin, boneless	4 lbs.	1.8 kg

Combine first 5 ingredients in a small bowl. Mix well.

Put pork tenderloin in a resealable freezer bag or container with a lid and pour marinade over. Allow pork to marinate in a cooler or refrigerator for at least 3 hours but preferably overnight. When ready to grill, place tenderloin on grill, turning regularly to avoid burning, until pork is cooked through and no longer pink, about 20 minutes.

꘡   When choosing a wood for kindling, cedar, in my opinion, is the best. Both white and red cedar is porous and contains natural oils, which help it burn fast and hot. Makes 6 servings.

Barbecue Baked Beans

The secret to great baked beans is to cook the beans at low heat for a relatively long time and ensure they've been soaked overnight before starting the slow-cooking process. They can be served alone with thick slices of fresh bread topped with mounds of butter, or as a side dish with steaks or ribs. The chilli sauce and Dijon mustard give this recipe a touch of heat.

Dried navy beans	2 cups	500 mL
Water	6 cups	1.5 L
Water	2 1/2 cups	625 mL
Cooking oil	1 tsp.	5 mL
Chopped onion	1 cup	250 mL
Garlic cloves, minced	2	2
Can of tomato sauce (14 oz., 398 mL)	1	1
Brown sugar, packed	1/3 cup	75 mL
Apple cider vinegar	1/4 cup	60 mL
Diced cooked bacon	1/4 cup	60 mL
Dijon mustard	1 tbsp.	15 mL
Worcestershire sauce	1 tbsp.	15 mL
Salt	1 tsp.	5 mL
Pepper	1/2 tsp.	2 mL

Put beans into a large bowl. Add first amount of water. Let stand, covered, for at least 8 hours or overnight. Drain and rinse beans.

Prepare campfire and heat a Dutch oven over hot coals. Put beans and second amount of water into Dutch oven.

Heat cooking oil in a small frying pan on medium. Add onion and garlic. Cook for 5 to 10 minutes, stirring occasionally, until onion is softened. Add to beans and cover. Use a small shovel to place about 15 hot coals on lid. Cook for about 2 hours.

Combine remaining 8 ingredients in a small bowl. Stir into Dutch oven and cook, covered, for about 30 minutes. Makes 7 servings.

Greek Pasta Camping Salad

This recipe requires virtually no campfire preparation and is an ideal side for any number of main courses in this book. The bulk of the salad can be prepared before you leave the house; simply stir and serve around the fire once your main course is ready to go.

Penne pasta	2 cups	500 mL
Olive oil	1/2 cup	125 mL
Red wine vinegar	1/4 cup	60 mL
Lemon juice	1 tbsp.	15 mL
Minced garlic	1 tsp.	10 mL
Dried oregano	2 tsp.	10 mL
Salt	1/4 tsp.	1 mL
Pepper	1/4 tsp.	1 mL
Cherry tomatoes, halved	10	10
Small red onion, chopped	1	1
Green pepper, chopped	1	1
Red pepper, chopped	1	1
Small cucumber, chopped	1	1
Feta cheese, crumbled	1/2 cup	125 mL
Black olives (optional)	1/2 cup	125 mL

Cook penne as per package directions. Once pasta has reached desired tenderness, remove from heat, drain and set aside.

For the vinaigrette, combine next 7 ingredients in a bowl and whisk until well mixed.

Combine next 7 ingredients in a large bowl or container and add pasta and vinaigrette. Cover and refrigerate until you are ready to use. Makes 5 servings.

Potato Salad with Dill

No picnic or outdoor gathering is complete without potato salad; whether your variation includes, egg, dill or lemon, you will likely not have any leftovers by the end of the meal. You can peel your potatoes or leave the skin on for this recipe; the salad is equally delicious either way.

Red potatoes	**10**	**10**
Sour cream	3/4 cup	175 mL
Mayonnaise	3/4 cup	175 mL
Apple cider vinegar	1 tbsp.	15 mL
Dijon mustard	1 tbsp.	15 mL
Small onion, diced	1/2	1/2
Celery rib, diced	1	1
Celery salt	1 tsp.	5 mL
Salt	1/2 tsp.	2 mL
Pepper	1/8 tsp.	0.5 mL
Hard-cooked eggs, diced	5	5
Fresh dill (or 1 tbsp., 15 mL, dillweed)	1/4 cup	60 mL

In a large pot, bring potatoes to a boil on high. Reduce heat to medium-low and cook until potatoes are cooked but still firm, about 20 minutes. Drain potatoes and set aside to cool. Once cool, cut potatoes into chunks.

For the dressing, combine next 9 ingredients in a medium bowl and mix well.

In a large bowl, combine potatoes, eggs, dressing and dried dill and mix lightly. Refrigerate until ready to use. Makes 5 servings.

～ For a bit of a change, or if you run out of vinegar, try substituting the vinegar with pickle juice.

Cheesy Pull Apart Garlic Bread

Is there any better pairing for homemade lasagna or spaghetti than homemade garlic bread? This campfire recipe with cheese adds some savoury goodness during a hot meal around the fire. For some reason it just tastes better cooked over an open fire that you built yourself.

Sourdough bread loaf	1	1
Butter	2 1/2 tbsp.	37 mL
Garlic cloves, minced	2	2
Grated mozzarella cheese	1 cup	250 mL
Chopped fresh parsley (optional)	2 tbsp.	30 mL

Cut loaf of bread in a crosshatch pattern or in slices, making sure not to cut right though to bottom. Spread butter deep into each slice and sprinkle garlic, cheese and parsley into each crevice. Wrap bread with aluminium foil and refrigerate or keep cold in cooler until ready to use. To cook, place bread in aluminium foil over your heat source for 15 to 20 minutes or until cheese has melted. Serve warm. Makes 4 servings.

Wilderness is not a luxury but a necessity of the human spirit, and as vital to our lives as water and good bread. —Edward Abbey

Homemade Snacking Beef Jerky

Commercial beef jerky is usually made with a dehydrator, but this homemade oven recipe does an excellent job just the same. Jerky is a fabulous food to carry along while backpacking because it keeps for such a long time and is easy and light to stow away in your hiking gear. Loaded with essential protein and fun to chew on while on the move, homemade beef jerky is one of the best snacks for backpacking.

Worcestershire sauce	3/4 cup	175 mL
Soy sauce	3/4 cup	175 mL
Smoked paprika	1 tbsp.	15 mL
Honey	1 tbsp.	15 mL
Pepper	2 tsp.	10 mL
Dried crushed chilies	1 tsp.	5 mL
Onion powder	1 tsp.	5 mL
Garlic powder	1 tsp.	5 mL
Beef sirloin tip roast, sliced thinly	2 lbs.	900 g

In a large bowl, whisk together first 8 ingredients.

Add beef and turn to coat. Cover bowl with plastic wrap and marinate in refrigerator for at least 3 hours. Line a baking sheet with aluminum foil and place a wire rack over foil. Transfer beef to paper towels to dry. Discard marinade. Arrange beef slices in a single layer on prepared wire rack. Bake beef in a 175°F (80°C) oven until dry and leathery, 3 to 4 hours. Cut into bite-size pieces and store in bags. Makes 30 pieces.

Fresh air and muddy boots make everything better.
—Unknown

Whole Grain Energy Bars

Energy bars are likely the most popular snack food among avid backpackers because of their nutrition and portability. This whole grain energy bar recipe is easy and tasty. One batch would provide a suitable snack option for two hikers for several days of backpacking.

Quinoa	1/2 cup	125 mL
Water	1 cup	250 mL
Vegetable oil	1/4 cup	60 mL
Vanilla	2 tsp.	10 mL
Quick-cooking rolled oats	2 cups	500 mL
Flaxseed meal	1/4 cup	60 mL
Protein powder	3/4 cup	175 mL
Baking soda	1 tsp.	5 mL
Sea salt	1/2 tsp.	2 mL
Walnut pieces	1/2 cup	125 mL
Raw sunflower seeds	1/2 cup	125 mL
Cranberries	1/2 cup	125 mL
Shredded coconut	1/2 cup	125 mL
Brown sugar	1/2 cup	125 mL
Whole wheat flour	1/2 cup	125 mL

Cook quinoa according to package directions.

Add water, oil and vanilla to quinoa.

Combine remaining 11 ingredients in a large bowl. Add wet ingredients to dry ingredients and stir to combine. Spread mixture into a greased 9 x 13 inch (23 x 33 cm) pan, pressing down firmly with your hands. Dough may seem slightly dry, but this is okay. Bake for 20 minutes at 350°F (175°C). Set aside to cool before cutting into bars. Wrap bars individually or place them in a container or resealable freezer bag. Makes 15 bars.

Homemade Trail Mix

Of course when you are making trail mix, you can mix and match ingredients.
This recipe is for a high protein version and includes chocolate, which could
potentially melt if you are in a hot environment. Feel free to substitute and
replace as you see fit.

Whole almonds	10	10
Whole cashews	10	10
Salted peanuts	10	10
Medium sweetened coconut	1 tbsp.	15 mL
Salted, roasted sunflower seeds	1 tbsp.	15 mL
Raw pumpkin seeds	1 tbsp.	15 mL
Dried cranberries	1 tbsp.	15 mL
Chocolate chips	1 tbsp.	15 mL

Combine all ingredients in a reusable container or resealable freezer bag.
Makes 1 serving.

When winter camping or hiking, keep your ready-to-eat items close to your body during the day so they aren't frozen when you want to eat them.

Returning home is the most difficult part of long-distance hiking; You have grown outside the puzzle and your piece no longer fits.
—Cindy Ross

Hiking Etiquette

As more people venture out into the great outdoors, there is the potential for the trails to get a bit crowded. Keep these few simple rules in mind to ensure that everyone has a safe and enjoyable wilderness experience.

First, watch out for other people on the trail. People enjoy the outdoors in many ways, whether on foot, mountain bike or horseback. If you encounter someone on horseback on the trail, step slowly off the trail and let them pass. Horse trumps hiker for right-of-way, partly because they are highly vigilant and easily spooked if approached too close, and partly because they are large animals that can trample you if you get underfoot.

People making their way uphill also have right-of-way over people who are descending. It takes a lot more energy to ascend a slope than it does to go down it, so it is best not to break someone's momentum by blocking their path or expecting them to step aside.

And, as on the city streets you've left behind by venturing into nature, slower traffic should keep to the right so that faster traffic can pass on the left. If you want to meander as you take in nature's beauty, best not to do it in the path of a fitness buff or outdoor warrior.

The next important rule of hiking is to leave no trace. This includes resisting the urge to leave your mark on trees, rocks and the like as well as keeping the impact of your passing to the bare minimum. If you are hiking an established trail, stay on it instead of tromping through the underbrush and crushing delicate vegetation. If you are in a pristine area in the backcountry, try to walk on surfaces where you will cause the least amount of disruption, such as gravel, rock or dry grass.

If "nature calls" and you are nowhere near the proper facilities, dig a hole at least 6 to 8 inches (15 to 20 cm) deep at least 200 feet (60 m) away from the trail, a campsite or a body of water, river or stream, and bury any solid waste.

And remember, whatever you pack in, you pack out; this includes toilet paper and all packaging from your food as well as food waste, even if it is biodegradable. Sure, blackened banana peels or rotting apple cores will eventually decompose, but until they do they can attract wildlife and make the trails less inviting to other people.

Another important rule is easily remembered by the old adage, "Take only memories, leave only footprints." Sure those wildflowers would look nice tucked behind your ear, or that rock would look great in your collection, but they look even better *in situ*, where they belong.

And last, if you are hiking with a dog, keep it on leash. First, it is just common courtesy. You know your people-loving pooch is as friendly as can be, but other people on the trail might not be comfortable with a dog running loose around them, especially if you are not nearby. More importantly, though, is the fact that dogs off leash in wilderness areas can get into trouble. The backcountry has all kinds of hazards for your unsuspecting pet, from unstable slopes or fast-moving streams to steep cliffs. And then there is the wildlife. Depending on where you are hiking, porcupines, bears, cougars, coyotes and wolves can all pose a threat to your dog. If your dog is being pursued by an aggressive animal and runs back to you for safety, you and your companions could also be at risk. Studies have shown that in recent years, the majority of bear attacks on humans were instigated by barking dogs.

These are only a few of the rules of hiking etiquette. For more information, check out online forums, or talk to local experts.

Campfire Pancakes

A hot meal like pancakes in the morning will be a welcome addition to any hiking trip and a wonderful way to start off a long day on the trail. Cold food and snacks are fine, but there's nothing quite like a hot home-cooked meal when roughing it in the backcountry!

All purpose flour	1 cup	250 mL
Baking powder	1 tsp.	5 mL
Baking soda	1/2 tsp.	2 mL
Dry milk powder	1 tbsp.	15 mL
Granulated sugar	1 tbsp.	15 mL
Water	2/3 cup	150 mL
Margarine	1 tbsp.	15 mL

Combine first 5 ingredients in a resealable freezer bag or other container.

To prepare pancakes, add water and margarine to bag. Squish bag to combine ingredients. Cut a corner off bag and squeeze mixture out into a hot frying pan. Cook until golden brown. Makes 4 pancakes.

How is it one careless match can start a forest fire, but it takes a whole box to start a campfire?
—Unknown

Strawberry Banana Granola

If you should be backpacking during wild berry season, feel free to replace the freeze-dried strawberries with wild berries you find along the way. Wild raspberries, blueberries and gooseberries are only a few types that may be available, depending on the season or region you're hiking in. Be sure you know what berries you have before you consume them.

High-protein granola	1/2 cup	125 mL
Freeze-dried strawberries	1/4 cup	60 mL
Banana chips	1/4 cup	60 mL
Brown sugar	2 tbsp.	30 mL
Dry whole milk powder	1/4 cup	60 mL
Water	1 cup	250 mL

Combine first 5 ingredients in a resealable freezer bag or other container.

To prepare granola, combine contents of bag with ingredients with water until milk powder has dissolved and fruits have rehydrated slightly. Makes 1 serving.

Set loose, a child would run down the paths, scramble up the rocks, lie on the earth. Grown-ups more often let their minds do the running, scrambling, and lying, but the emotion is shared. It feels good to be here.
—David Miller, AWOL on the Appalachian Trail

Backpacker Stew

The amount of food a backpacker require varies greatly depending on whom you ask. The general rule, based on caloric intake for an average day of backpacking is 3000 calories for men and 2000 calories for women. For a more strenuous day of backpacking, men may require 4000 calories and women about 3000. Estimating the amount and type of extra food to carry on a long hiking trip can be a fine science, as the backpacker needs to consider the weight versus nutritional value for each item. For this one-pot backpacker stew, opt for an aluminum cooking pot instead of the heavier Dutch oven if you are concerned about weight.

Ground beef	1 lb.	454 g
Mixed vegetables	2 cups	500 mL
Can of condensed tomato soup	1	1
(10 oz., 284 mL)		
Can of condensed vegetable beef soup	1	1
(10 oz., 284 mL)		
Water	1/4 cup	60 mL
Garlic powder	1/4 tsp.	1 mL
Onion powder	1/4 tsp.	1 mL
Salt	1/4 tsp.	1 mL
Pepper	1/4 tsp.	1 mL

In a cast iron pot or Dutch oven positioned 1 or 2 inches (2.5 to 5 cm) above a hot bed of coals, cook ground beef until no longer pink, and then drain. Stir in remaining ingredients, cover and simmer for 30 minutes or until heated through. Serve with fresh bread or bannock. Makes 4 servings.

Of all the paths you take in life, make sure a few of them are dirt.
—John Muir

Chicken and Cashew Curry Rice

This quick and easy recipe is perfect for backpackers. Simply add all the ingredients to a resealable bag throw the bag in your pack. When you arrive at your destination, all you need is a campfire and some fresh water, and you have a hearty meal.

Instant brown rice	2/3 cup	150 mL
Freeze-dried chicken	1/4 cup	60 mL
Chopped cashews	1/4 cup	60 mL
Freeze-dried mixed vegetables	1/4 cup	60 mL
Chicken bouillon powder	1 1/2 tsp.	7 mL
Curry powder	1 1/2 tsp.	7 mL
Onion flakes	1 tsp.	5 mL
Garlic powder	1/4 tsp.	1 mL
Salt	1/4 tsp.	1 mL
Pepper	1/8 tsp.	0.5 mL
Water	1 1/2 cups	375 mL

Combine first 10 ingredients in a resealable freezer bag or other container.

To cook, bring water to a boil. Pour contents of bag into a small pot or bowl and pour boiling water over top. Cover and let rest for 10 minutes, stirring once or twice to mix ingredients, until ingredients have rehydrated. Makes 1 serving.

The antidote to exhaustion isn't rest. It's nature.
—Shikoba

Campers' Creamy Chicken Alfredo

This is another quick and easy backpacking recipe to bring along with you on your next trip. Because it takes so little advanced preparation, it will free up your time to research the trails you plan on hiking. For safety reasons, knowing the most about your backpacking destination is essential. Speak to other hikers who've travelled that route in the past to determine how difficult it is and whether you or your party will require any special equipment or resources. The Internet is a wonderful resource, and many hiking forums and chat groups include information and tips on a variety of backpacking trails in Canada.

Small egg noodles	1 cup	250 mL
Freeze-dried chicken	1/4 cup	60 mL
Pine nuts, toasted	1/4 cup	60 mL
Freeze-dried mushrooms	1/4 cup	60 mL
Chicken bouillon powder	1 1/2 tsp.	7 mL
Grated Parmesan cheese	3 tbsp.	45 mL
Powdered milk	2 tbsp.	30 mL
Corn starch	2 tbsp.	30 mL
Italian seasoning	3/4 tsp.	4 mL
Garlic powder	1/4 tsp.	1 mL
Pepper	1/8 tsp.	0.5 mL
Salt	1/4 tsp.	1 mL
Water	1 1/4 cups	300 mL

Combine first 12 ingredients in a resealable freezer bag or other container.

To cook, bring water to a boil. Pour contents of bag into a small pot or bowl and pour boiling water over top. Cover and let rest for 10 minutes, stirring once or twice to mix ingredients, until ingredients have rehydrated. Makes 1 serving.

Couscous with Spicy Tuna

Another easy backpacking meal that requires only a small campfire, enough to boil water, and you're all set. Remember that even the smallest campfire needs to be treated careful so as not to spread or send embers astray, which can be dangerous during the dry season. Even small campfires less than 12 inches (30 cm) in diameter need to be fully extinguished before you exit the area and move on. Dozens of forest fires are started each year from campers being careless.

Couscous	1/3 cup	75 mL
Freeze-dried mixed vegetables	2 tbsp.	30 mL
Water	1 cup	250 mL
Can of Thai chili tuna (5 oz., 140 g)	1	1

Put couscous and freeze-dried vegetables in a resealable freezer bag or container.

To cook, bring water to a boil. Pour contents of bag into a small pot or bowl and pour boiling water over. Cover and let rest for 10 minutes, stirring once or twice to mix ingredients, until ingredients have rehydrated. Drain off any excess water. Add tuna just before serving and wix well. Makes 1 serving.

Couscous is typically sold in two forms: Israeli couscous, which is white and pea sized, and African couscous, which is yellow and significantly smaller. Look for the African form for this recipe.

Hikers' Lentil Stew

Any of the backpacking recipes that are prepared in advance and stored in a sealed bag have but two essential requirements: a cooking pot and water. The best cooking pot is light and easily storable along with your hiking equipment. Some manufacturers make an ergonomic set of cooking pots of different size that fit inside one another for easy storage. Depending on your weight limitations, however, you may opt for just one cooking pot and a limited number of utensils. Lentils are tasty and nutritious and very popular among outdoor enthusiasts. Double or triple the recipe to serve more people and adjust the cooking time accordingly.

Red lentils	6 tbsp.	90 mL
Vegetable bouillon cube	1	1
Onion flakes	1 tsp.	5 mL
Garlic flakes	1 tsp.	5 mL
Dried bay leaf	1	1
Dried thyme	1/2 tsp.	2 mL
Dried rosemary, crushed	1/4 tsp.	1 mL
Dried oregano	1/4 tsp.	1 mL
Pepper	1/8 tsp.	0.5 mL
Cumin	1/8 tsp.	0.5 mL
Chili Flakes	1/8 tsp.	0.5 mL
Water	2 1/2 cups	625 mL

Add first 11 ingredients to a resealable bag or container. Label bag or container to remember what is in it.

When you are ready to eat, simply empty your bag or container into a cooking pot and add water. Place pot on heat source and bring to a boil, stirring frequently. Allow to cook for about 20 minutes or until lentils have reached desired tenderness. Makes 1 serving.

Not all who wander are lost.
—J.R.R. Tolkien

Healthy Quinoa Stew with Peppers

You may not realize it, but quinoa is likely one of the most nutritious foods you can eat. It is loaded with protein and contains nearly twice as much fibre as other grains. It is also a good source of magnesium, iron and riboflavin. One top of its health benefits, quinoa has become a trendy health food item in recent years. So if you want to backpack in style and keep up with recent trends while eating healthy, this is this is the recipe for you.

Quinoa (cooked and dehydrated)	1/3 cup	75 mL
Dried roasted red peppers	3 tbsp.	45 mL
Cilantro	1 tbsp.	15 mL
Tomato powder	1 tbsp.	15 mL
Sun dried tomatoes, chopped	1 tbsp.	15 mL
Dried mixed vegetables	1 tbsp.	15 mL
Dried oregano	1/2 tsp.	2 mL
Vegetable bouillon powder	1/2 tsp.	2 mL
Garlic powder	1/4 tsp.	1 mL

Combine all ingredients in a resealable freezer bag. When ready to eat, pour contents into a cup and add enough hot water to cover. Stir and set aside for 5 minutes or until the vegetables are rehydrated. Stir well and eat. Makes 1 serving.

Remember when preparing your ingredients in the resealable freezer bag to label the bag with the meal name and cooking instructions. You may not remember the cooking instructions by the time you are ready to prepare your food.

Cheesy Mashed Potatoes

This terrific backpacking potato recipe makes a perfect side for a number of mains. The only thing better than regular mashed potatoes to stick to your ribs, as my Dad used to say, is mashed potatoes fancied-up with cheese and vegetables.

Instant mashed potatoes	2 cups	500 mL
Freeze-dried broccoli	1 cup	250 mL
Minced onion	1 tbsp.	15 mL
Powdered Cheddar cheese	1/3 cup	75 mL
Salt	1/2 tsp.	2 mL
Pepper	1/8 tsp	0.5 mL
Powdered butter	2 tbsp.	30 mL
Water	2 cups	500 mL
Olive oil	2 tbsp.	30 mL

Combine first 7 ingredients in a resealable freezer bag or other container.

To cook, heat up water. Place contents of freezer bag in a bowl or pot. Carefully pour hot water into dry ingredients, a little at a time, stirring as you go until potatoes have reached desired consistency (you may not use all the water). Cover and let rest for 2 to 3 minutes.

Stir in olive oil and enjoy. Makes 1 serving.

Many well-stocked supermarkets will carry powdered Cheddar cheese but if you can't find it in your local store, check online. It is readily available on the Internet.

Building the Perfect Campfire for Cooking

The first step in building the perfect cooking fire is finding the perfect firewood. The ideal wood for cooking fires is dry hardwood and softwood kindling. Green wood is not suitable; it makes for a smoky, smouldering mess and can give your food an unpleasant taste and smell. Suitable split hardwood, such as maple, yellow birch, beach, oak or elm will work nicely along with a bag or small box full of dried split kindling. Red or white cedar is the best kindling, but pine and spruce will do. Kindling wood should be split into thin pieces (about 1 inch, 2.5 cm) pieces with a small splitting axe or hatchet.

The most appropriate location for a campfire is in a designated fire pit surrounded by rocks; or you can build your fire on a flat rock so that no surrounding debris can catch fire. Always try to use an established fire pit if there is one at your campsite; it's a good way to minimize your impact on the site you're using. If possible, gather 10 to 12 rocks that are 10 to 12 inches (25 to 30 cm) in diameter and arrange them in a circle to encompass your fire pit. On windy days, be careful that your embers don't scatter, or they could ignite a fire somewhere else. As for the fire pit itself, if you can locate a large rock, place it toward the wind with the rest of the pit behind. This will help your fire get a good start and will funnel the smoke in one direction while you're cooking.

Once you've chosen your fire pit location, crumple several sheets of newsprint and place them at the bottom of the pit. I find the cage design campfire works best: lay two small (3 to 4 inch, 7.5 to 10 cm, diameter) hardwood pieces parallel to each other about 12 to 18 inches (30 to 45 cm) apart, depending on the size of your pit. Assemble a handful of dry kindling and lay it across the paper running in the opposite direction to the hardwood sticks, forming a makeshift cage design. Place two more hardwood sticks opposite to the first two and then add one small hardwood sticks across the top diagonally. The cage fire design allows for maximum airflow and will combust very quickly.

Ignite your fire by lighting the paper, and keep an eye on the kindling to make sure it is starting to burn. As the fire progresses, gently lay 3 or 4 more hardwood pieces in the flames one at a time. Once the fire has burned down and a bed of coals appears, use a green stick or fire poker to smooth out the coals for cooking. Now you are ready to place the cooking grid or grate across the coals and start cooking.

Hunt Camp Breakfast Quiche

This traditional breakfast quiche is equally at home around the open fire as it is at a hunt camp. It is a savoury breakfast meal hearty enough to satisfy a camp full of hungry hunters, but also works as a simple breakfast to be enjoyed by the glow of a campfire with a small gathering of friends. Dig in and enjoy!

Bacon slices, diced	1/2 lb.	225 g
Medium onion, diced	1	1
Ground pork sausage	1/2 lb.	225 g
Eggs	12	12
Bag frozen diced hash browns (2 lbs., 900 g)	1	1
Grated Cheddar cheese	2 cups	500 mL
Fresh dill (or 1 1/2 tsp. dillweed), optional	1 tbsp	15 mL

Prepare campfire and preheat Dutch oven on a grid 2 or 3 inches (2.5 or 7.5 cm) above hot coals. Brown bacon and onion in Dutch oven; drain bacon fat. Add ground sausage and hash browns and cook for 15 minutes until potatoes begin to brown.

Meanwhile, beat eggs together in bowl. Pour over bacon mixture and cook for 10 to 15 minutes until eggs have started to set. Sprinkle cheese and dill over eggs. Cook until eggs are set completely and cheese has melted. Slice and serve. Makes 6 servings.

I would feel more optimistic about a bright future for man if he spent less time proving that he can outwit Nature and more time tasting her sweetness and respecting her seniority.
—E.B. White

Breakfast Kebabs

As the fog lifts off the lake and you hear the distant call of the loon, your first campfire of the day crackles with anticipation. Getting breakfast started before anyone is awake is a secret passion of mine, but I don't often admit that because people would think I'm nuts. Whether it's traditional eggs and bacon or these fun breakfast kebabs, there is something special about preparing breakfast with the cool morning air in your lungs. And there is no better way to build a strong appetite! You could prepare the sauce in advance at home to make things a little easier at the campsite.

Baby potatoes, unpeeled, cut in half	3	3
Cherry tomatoes	6	6
Pineapple cubes (1 inch, 2.5 cm, pieces)	6	6
Bacon slices	6	6
Red pepper, cut in 1 inch (2.5 cm) pieces	1/2	1/2
Green pepper, cut in 1 inch (2.5 cm) pieces	1/2	1/2
Yellow pepper, cut in 1 inch (2.5 cm) pieces	1/2	1/2
Mushrooms	6	6
Strawberries, ends trimmed	6	6
Ketchup	1/4 cup	60 mL
Balamic vinegar	2 tbsp.	30 mL
Soy sauce	1 tbsp.	15 mL
Dijon mustard	1 tbsp.	15 mL
Honey	1 tbsp.	15 mL
Worcestershire sauce	1 tsp.	5 mL
Cayenne pepper	1/2 tsp.	2 mL
Lemon juice	1 tsp.	5 mL

Fill a medium saucepan with enough water to cover potatoes. Cook on a grid placed about 2 inches (5 cm) over hot coals until potatoes are almost tender, about 10 minutes. Drain and set aside to cool.

Arrange ingredients on skewers in the following order: potato half, cherry tomato, pineapple, bacon, red pepper, green pepper, yellow pepper, mushroom and strawberry.

For sauce, combine remaining 8 ingredients in a small bowl. Brush skewers with sauce and cook until heated through, turning and brushing with sauce several times. Makes 6 skewers.

Outdoor Breakfast Burritos

Breakfast burritos are popular with people on the go because they are tasty, nutritious and very portable. The same convenience holds true when making them outdoors. Sometimes I'll make extras and wrap them in aluminum foil to put in my pocket as a snack for later on down the trail.

Large potato	1	1
Breakfast sausage, crumbled	1/2 cup	125 mL
Green onion or shallot, sliced	1	1
Salt	1/8 tsp.	0.5 mL
Pepper	1/8 tsp.	0.5 mL
Eggs, lightly beaten	4	4
Flour tortillas (9 inch, 23 cm, diameter)	2	2
Grated Cheddar cheese	1/2 cup	125 mL
Salsa (optional)	1/4 cup	60 mL

Peel, chop and parboil your potato until just tender but not falling apart.

In a cast iron pan, cook ground sausage until browned.

Stir in potatoes, green onions, salt and pepper. Cook, stirring occasionally, until heated through.

Add eggs and cook until scrambled.

Meanwhile, lay out 2 large squares of foil (about 16 inches, 40 cm) and place a tortilla on each. Divide egg mixture between both tortillas and sprinkle each with cheese.

Fold bottom and sides of tortillas over filling and wrap each in foil and place over campfire. Cook your burritos, flipping once, about 5 minutes per side (depending on the heat of your campfire) until cheese is melted and burrito is heated completely through. Serve with salsa, if desired. Makes 2 servings.

Burritos are a Mexican dish that traditionally consisted of only meat and refried beans. They have evolved into different variations over the years with a variety of ingredients being used. The word burrito means "little donkey" in Spanish.

Off the Beaten Path Pie Iron French Toast

Not your traditional French toast, this recipe is a delicious treat in the morning for breakfast or as a snack later in the day while sitting around the campfire. A pie iron is a highly useful campfire cooking implement and should be carried on every outdoor adventure. Serve with maple syrup or enjoy as is!

Butter	1 tbsp.	15 mL
Slices of cinnamon raisin bread	2	2
Cream cheese	1 tbsp.	15 mL
Banana, sliced	1	1
Chopped walnuts (optional)	1 tsp.	5 mL

Heat pie iron and spray with cooking spray or grease with melted butter. Butter outside of each slice of bread and place 1 slice on pie iron. Spread cream cheese onto bread. Arrange banana slices over cheese and sprinkle with walnuts. Top with second slice of bread, keeping butter on outside. Cook until browned, about 3 minutes per side. Makes 1 sandwich.

☙ Be sure to extinguish your campfire with water before leaving the area or going to bed. Pour water on it and once the ashes no longer hiss, it should no longer burn or pose a safety hazard.

Only one who wanders finds a new path.
—Norwegian Proverb

Corned Beef Hash and Eggs

Once you get past the stigma of the corned beef and hash component of this recipe, the end result is very tasty and thoroughly satisfying. There's just something fulfilling about cooking even the most basic recipe over a fire you built yourself.

Diced cooked peeled potato (about 1/4 inch, 6 mm pieces)	2 cups	500 mL
Cooked corned beef, cut into chunks	1 lb.	454 g
Finely chopped onion	1/2 cup	125 mL
Milk	1 1/2 tbsp.	22 mL
Pepper	1/4 tsp.	1 mL
Butter	1 tbsp.	15 mL
Large eggs	4	4
Chopped fresh parsley	3 tbsp.	45 mL
Salt, to taste		

Combine first 5 ingredients in a medium bowl.

Melt butter in a cast iron skillet placed 1 to 2 inches (2.5 to 5 cm) above hot coals. Stir in corned beef mixture. Cook, covered, for about 15 minutes, stirring occasionally, until heated through. Cook, uncovered, for about 35 minutes, stirring occasionally, until browned.

Make 4 holes in hash and break 1 egg into each. Cook, covered, for about 5 minutes, or until eggs are cooked to desired doneness. Sprinkle with parsley and salt. Makes 4 servings.

Rugged Cast Iron Breakfast Potatoes

Although cumbersome, the cast iron skillet should be part of any campfire cooking trip. The number of meals you can cook in this trusty skillet is limitless. Good used cast iron cookware can be readily found at many thrift stores and is an economical way to build your campfire cookware inventory. When shopping for a good cast iron skillet, examine the cooking surface closely and avoid pans with deep scratches, rusting or pitting. A well-maintained cast iron skillet will appear smooth and be a rich black colour.

Olive oil	2 tbsp.	30 mL
Butter	2 tbsp.	30 mL
Medium onion, chopped	1	1
Medium potatoes, cubed	6	6
Medium green pepper, diced	1	1
Jalapeño pepper, chopped	1	1
Olive oil	2 tbsp.	30 mL
Water	1/4 cup	60 mL
Garlic powder	2 tsp.	10 mL
Paprika	1 tsp.	5 mL
Salt	2 tsp.	10 mL
Pepper	1 tsp.	5 mL

Heat first amount olive oil and butter in a cast iron skillet or frying pan on grill over campfire. Add onion and cook until softened.

Add potato, green pepper, jalapeño pepper and remaining 2 tbsp. (30 mL) oil, and cook, stirring frequently, until potatoes start to brown.

Add water and cook, covered, for about 5 minutes so potatoes can steam.

Add remaining 4 ingredients and cook, stirring frequently, until potatoes have browned and are tender. Makes 4 servings.

~ In 2010, English farmer Peter Glazebrook grew the world's biggest potato, which weighed a hefty 8 1/4 lbs. (3.76 kg). Just imagine the meals that would produce!

Rustic Croque-Monsieur

The croque-monsieur is a traditional French ham and cheese sandwich composed of sourdough bread, Cheddar cheese and any of several types of ham. The beauty of a croque-monsieur cooked over the open fire is the deliciously smoky flavour of the melted cheese and heated ham. It is simply melt-in-your-mouth good! To make this dish a little more rustic, we've swapped the sourdough for white bread (though you can use whatever type of bread you prefer) and have forgone the usual pie iron, opting instead for a trusty stick. Nothing says "roughing it" like food cooked on a stick over a campfire.

White bread slices	4	4
Butter	2 tbsp.	30 mL
Cheddar cheese slices	4	4
Smoked ham slices (1/4 inch, 6 mm, thick)	2	2

Prepare campfire. Butter 1 side of 2 slices of bread. Lay 1 slice of bread flat (butter-side down) on a two-pronged stick whittled from a green sapling. Add 2 slices of cheese and 1 slice of ham. Hold over hot coals and toast slowly. When cheese has melted and bread is lightly toasted, add second slice of bread (butter-side up) and turn over to toast. Repeat for second sandwich. Makes 2 sandwiches.

൜ Choose a stick from a green sapling to make your sandwich because it won't catch on fire.

Campfire Cooking Essentials

There are a few small items and cooking utensils one should always have when travelling into the backwoods. Here are just a few essential items every outdoor chef should have on hand at all times: copious amounts of aluminum foil, non-stick cooking spray, skewers (metal and wood), oven mitts or pot holders, a fire igniter, extra cooking oil, paper towels, a paring knife, a fillet knife, a meat saw, scissors, an axe, a shovel and a camping cooler.

When cooking over a campfire, we generally use what is referred to as a cooking "grid" or "grate," which is basically a portable cooking grill similar to the cooking surface of a gas barbecue. Properly positioning your campfire grid over the coals is very important. A small handful of baseball-sized rocks positioned around the coals make a great support for your cooking grid. A good height from the coals is typically 2 to 3 inches (5 to 7.5 cm), unless the recipe calls for more or less clearance.

The mighty Dutch oven is another campfire must. Basically just an oversized pot with a lid, the Dutch oven comes in variety of colours and configurations, but all share one common trait: they are made of cast iron. Some are enamelled, whereas other types are not. This cast iron construction retains heat extremely well, making the Dutch oven an ideal cooking pot for a wide range of campfire cooking recipes.

Another useful campfire cooking tool is the tripod or spit. Tripods are usually constructed with three long metal legs splayed apart, with the tripod center point hanging directly above the campfire. A metal wire or chain with a hook on the bottom is suspended from the tripod allowing cooking pots to hang directly above the fire. A tripod is used as a replacement for a cooking grill or grate, if none is available.

Another useful item is a prepared portable spice kit. First decide which spices you cannot live without (my seven essential spices are salt, pepper, allspice, garlic powder, oregano, chilli powder and parsley). Then choose a small plastic or metal waterproof container (small candy tubes or metal mint tins with sealable tops work best to keep moisture and critters from spoiling the spices). Next you'll need to cut seven straws to a length slightly shorter than your spice container. Seal one end of the straws with tape, gently sprinkle your spices into the straw tubes, and close the other end off with another small piece of tape. Place the straws in your waterproof container. Your spice kit will prove invaluable for any cooking you do in the great outdoors, whether you are backpacking through remote Canadian wildness or spending the weekend at a campground a kilometre away from home. I prepare two spice kits in advance just in case one should get lost.

Enjoy your campfire this summer, and happy cooking!

Great Outdoors Beef Stroganoff

There is just something about the great outdoors that builds a healthy appetite. The body's reaction to fresh air and outdoor physical activity probably has something to do with it. Hearty meals like one this fit right in when camping or relaxing outdoors.

Beef sirloin steak, cut into strips	3/4 lb.	340 g
Large onion, sliced	1	1
Sliced fresh white mushrooms	1 cup	250 mL
Beef broth	2 cups	500 mL
Water	1 cup	250 mL
Can of condensed cream of chicken soup (10 oz., 284 mL)	1	1
Egg noodles	2 1/2 cups	625 mL
Worcestershire sauce	1 tbsp.	15 mL
Pepper	1/4 tsp.	1 mL
Sour cream	3/4 cup	175 mL

In a skillet, on a grill placed 2 or 3 inches (5 or 7.5 cm) over your campfire, fry beef until browned, stirring often to prevent sticking. Transfer to a medium bowl and set aside.

Add onion and mushrooms to skillet and cook for 3 minutes. Remove from heat and combine with beef in bowl. Set aside.

Combine broth, water and soup in skillet. Bring to a boil and add egg noodles. Reduce heat to a gentle boil and cook, stirring often, until noodles are tender. Add Worcestershire sauce and pepper. Simmer for 5 minutes.

Return beef mixture to skillet and heat gently. Stir in sour cream and heat through, but do not boil. Makes 4 servings.

Fireside Beef Nachos

Nachos are great for passing around the fire among large groups of people on any outdoor adventure. Easy to prepare and fun to cook in the great outdoors, this recipe will quickly become a campfire cooking mainstay. Top with your choice of fixings, such as jalapeños, sour cream and guacamole.

Vegetable oil	1 tbsp.	15 mL
Onion, chopped	1/2	1/2
Red pepper, chopped (optional)	1/2	1/2
Ground beef	1 lb.	454 g
Black beans	1/2 cup	125 mL
Envelope of taco seasoning (1 1/4 oz., 35 g)	1	1
Bag of tortilla chips	1	1
Grated mozzarella or Cheddar cheese	2 cups	500 mL
Salsa	1 cup	250 mL

In a skillet, on a grill over your campfire, heat oil and sauté onion and bell peppers until soft.

Add ground beef and taco seasoning and cook according to package directions (add water if package directions call for it.) Add black beans. Once beef is cooked thoroughly, drain and set aside.

Spray one side of 6 large sheets of aluminum foil (about 16 inches, 40 cm, long) with cooking spray. Spread tortilla chips in centre of each foil sheet and top with ground beef mixture and cheese. Fold in sides of tinfoil to seal so steam cannot escape. Cook on campfire grill for approximately 10 minutes. Remove carefully and enjoy. Serve with salsa. Makes 6 servings.

༄ For an incredible pair of outdoor cooking gloves, visit your local hardware store and purchase a pair of welding gloves. They protect your hands from the heat of a campfire and are long enough to cover your forearms so they don't get singed.

Backwoods Stuffed Onions

This interesting twist on stuffed peppers will have you coming back for more! To ease the campfire cooking process and allow yourself more time to enjoy the social aspect of camping, you could prepare the meat mixture and other ingredients before you leave home. If you have any fresh herbs on hand, sprinkle them over the cooked onions to add a splash of colour.

Large sweet onion	4	4
Ground beef	1 lb.	454 g
Garlic cloves, minced	3	3
Dried basil	1 tbsp.	15 mL
Dried oregano	1 tbsp.	15 mL
Dried parsley	1 tbsp.	15 mL
Salt	1/2 tsp.	2 mL
Pepper	1/2 tsp.	2 mL
Egg, lightly beaten	1	1
Fresh bread crumbs	1/2 cup	125 mL
Milk	1/2 cup	125 mL
Grated Parmesan cheese	1 cup	250 mL

Slice off top 1/4 of onions, and slice roots from bottom so onions sit flat without rolling over. Peel skins from onions. Cut an "X" into centre of each onion and scoop out centre portion with a spoon, leaving walls approximately 1/2 inch thick. Dice centres.

Combine 1/4 cup (60 mL) diced onion with remaining 11 ingredients (reserve remaining diced onion for another use). Stuff beef mixture into onions and place tops back on onions. Wrap onions in large squares of foil, bringing seams together on top by flattening the foil slightly. Keep wrapped onions upright and nestle each on hot coals. With a small shovel, top each onion with 1 to 2 hot coals. Cook for approximately 30 minutes, or until a meat thermometer inserted into centre registers 175°F (80°C). Remove from coals, carefully open foil and serve. Makes 4 servings.

ᴄᴠ Aluminium foil makes a great scouring pad for your dirty camp dishes. Just crumple up some foil and use it as a scrubber on those cast iron frying pans. It does a super job.

Build Your Own Shish Kebabs

This recipe allows dinner guests to enjoy the veggies and meat of their choice. I sometimes double up the peppers and onions and leave the mushrooms out altogether, whereas others may prefer extra mushrooms and no onions. Or maybe some guests would prefer chicken or pork instead of beef. That's the beauty of build your own. Everybody is left satisfied, even the finicky eaters.

Red wine vinegar	1/2 cup	125 mL
Vegetable oil	1/2 cup	125 mL
Parsley flakes	1 tbsp.	15 mL
Minced garlic	1 tsp.	5 mL
Salt	1/2 tsp.	2 mL
Pepper	1/2 tsp.	2 mL
Sirloin beef (or pork tenderloin), cut into 3/4 inch (2 cm) cubes	2 lbs.	900 g
Whole fresh white mushrooms	8 oz.	225 g
Red pepper, cut into chunks	1	1
Green pepper, cut into chunks	1	1
Zucchini, cubed	1	1
Cherry tomatoes	2 cups	500 mL

Combine red wine vinegar, vegetable oil, parsley flakes, garlic, salt and pepper in a small bowl. Transfer 3/4 of marinade to a resealable freezer bag or airtight container and add beef cubes. Transfer remaining 1/4 of marinade to another resealable freezer bag or container and add mushrooms. Allow meat and mushrooms to marinate, refrigerated, until ready to use.

To cook, thread your skewers with your choice of vegetables and meat. Brush leftover marinade over skewered vegetables to add some flavour.

Place shish kebabs on grill over fire and cook until meat has reached desired doneness, about 10 minutes. Makes 4 to 6 servings.

When debating whether to use metal and wood skewers, remember that wooden skewers can catch fire, whereas metal skewers heat faster and help to cook your food more thoroughly.

One-skillet Wilderness Cassoulet

The cassoulet originated from the Toulouse region of France and remains popular today. Basic cassoulet recipes include only beans and pork, whereas others might include mutton, lamb, goose or duck. In the province of Quebec, the cassoulet reigns supreme and is served a million different ways. For the camper and backpacker, there's nothing wrong with a bit of more refined French cuisine now and again.

Vegetable oil	1 tbsp.	15 mL
Carrots, diced	2	2
Celery ribs, diced	2	2
Small onion, diced	1	1
Garlic cloves, minced	2	2
Smoked sausage, diced	1/2 lb.	225 g
Can of red kidney beans (14 oz., 398 mL), drained and rinsed	1	1
Can of white kidney beans (14 oz., 398 mL) drained and rinsed	1	1
Can of diced tomatoes (with juice) (14 oz., 398 mL)	1	1
Bay leaves	2	2
Dried thyme	1 tsp.	5 mL
Dried crushed chilies	1/2 tsp.	2 mL
Salt	1/2 tsp.	2 mL
Pepper	1/2 tsp.	2 mL

Heat oil in a large cast iron skillet about 2 inches (5 cm) over coals. Add carrots, celery, onion and garlic and cook, stirring, for a few minutes, until onion is softened.

Add sausage to skillet and cook for a few more minutes to brown.

Add kidney beans and tomatoes, and season with bay leaves, thyme, chilies, salt and pepper. Cover and raise skillet to 4 inches (10 cm) above coals. Simmer for 15 minutes, stirring occasionally. Remove and discard bay leaves before serving. Makes 4 servings.

Campfire Pizza

This recipe calls for a pizza stone, which mimics the effects of cooking a pizza in a masonry oven. The porous nature of the stone helps absorb moisture, resulting in a crispy crust. You can find a pizza stone at many outdoor outfitter stores, or you might even find a suitable piece of flat slate rock around your campsite that might work.

Refrigerated pizza dough	1 lb.	454 g
Pizza sauce	1/4 cup	60 mL
Grated mozzarella cheese	1/2 cup	125 mL
Pepperoni slices	15	15

Roll out pizza dough to your desired thickness and place on a pizza stone. Place pizza stone on grill directly over campfire. Cook until bottom side of dough is golden brown, approximately 10 minutes.

Remove pizza stone from fire and flip dough over. Spread pizza sauce evenly on cooked side of dough. Sprinkle mozzarella cheese over sauce and top with pepperoni slices. Cover loosely with foil and cook until cheese has melted, about 10 minutes more. Remove pizza from stone and allow to cool slightly before slicing. Makes 4 servings.

When collecting wood for your campfire cooking, remember to use only dry wood to produce the cleanest-burning fire. Green branches off trees will burn poorly, produce unnecessary pollution and result in unpleasant tasting food.

Lemon Herb Lamb Chops

Though lamb is not as popular as other campfire meats, it is a nice treat now and again. Always make sure when cooking lamb, or any meats over the campfire, that the bed of coals is sufficient in depth to produce ample heat for at minimum of 20 to 30 minutes of cooking time. A thin bed of mostly softwood coals will likely fizzle out half through, which would spell disaster for the entire meal.

Lemon juice	3 tbsp.	45 mL
Finely grated lemon zest	1 tsp.	5 mL
Parsley flakes	1 tbsp.	15 mL
Liquid honey	1 tbsp.	15 mL
Dried oregano	1/2 tsp.	2 mL
Dried crushed chilies	3/4 tsp.	4 mL
Olive oil	3 tbsp.	45 mL
Salt	1/2 tsp.	2 mL
Pepper	1/4 tsp.	1 mL
Garlic cloves, minced	2	2
Lamb chops (about 1 lb., 454 g)	8	8

Combine first 10 ingredients in a medium resealable freezer bag.

Add lamb chops and turn to coat. Seal bag and marinate in cooler or refrigerator for at least 6 hours or overnight, turning occasionally. Drain and discard marinade. Once your campfire has burned down to a suitable bed of hot coals, place your cooking grid 2 inches (5 cm) above coals. Place lamb chops on grid evenly positioned over middle of hot coals. Cook chops for about 10 minutes, turning often to prevent burning, until centre is pink. Makes 4 servings.

Safe Campsite Food Storage

When you are camping and cooking in the great outdoors, whether it be in a campground a few kilometres from home or deep in the backcountry, you need to properly store your food supply. There are many creatures that would love to help themselves to the contents of your cooler. Animals are on a constant hunt for food, and they will take the path of least resistance. An unattended picnic table, backpack or cooler is a virtual buffet for any animal that tracks it down.

This may not be a big deal if the food thief is a whisky jack stealing a piece of bacon out of your frying pan, or a squirrel stealing a sandwich out of your pack, but much more dangerous if it is a bear wandering into your camp or rummaging through your tent. Where proper food storage is concerned, the rules are the same for large predators as they are for say a chipmunk or raccoon.

Adopting scrupulously clean practices and proper food storage will lower your chances of a negative wildlife encounter. Always keep your food supply stowed far away from your sleeping area. Limiting the scrap food around your camp will lower the chances of an animal entering your campsite. Do not bring so much as a stick of gum into your tent after dark. Any sort of food or sweet-smelling items can attract unwanted guests to your tent. In bear country, this includes such items as toothpaste, deodorant and soap.

The best food storage location in the frontcountry is locked away in the trunk of your car or inside the back seat of your SUV or truck. Food storage containers and coolers may be brought to the campfire-area during meal preparation and dinner but must be returned the safe area immediately afterward. If you are camping in the backcountry, string your backpack up in a tree away from your tent site. The branch you choose should be sturdy enough to support your pack but not so strong that a bear could climb out on it; and the backpack should be far enough out on the branch so that an enterprising bear cannot reach it by climbing up the trunk.

Viewing wildlife in its natural environment can be one of the most rewarding parts of camping, but you must be mindful that you are in their home, and the burden of responsibility rests on you to keep yourself, and ultimately the animals, safe. As the saying goes, "A fed bear is dead bear." Animals that have been fed once at a site, even inadvertently, will return to that site in search of food, which can put you, the animals and future campers at risk of an unwanted and unsafe encounter.

Smoky Bacon Drumsticks

Bacon is the perfect moist covering in this smoky drumsticks recipe. As it renders, the bacon's natural juices are exchanged in a perfect marriage of chicken and pork. With the skin removed from the chicken, the bacon strips make this recipe much more campfire-friendly, and lot yummier!

Smoked sweet paprika	1 tbsp.	15 mL
Garlic powder	1 tsp.	5 mL
Salt	1 tsp.	5 mL
Pepper	1/2 tsp.	2 mL
Chicken drumstick (about 3 oz., 85 g, each), skin removed	12	12
Bacon slices	12	12
Vegetable oil	2 tsp.	10 mL

Combine first 4 ingredients in a small cup.

Rub paprika mixture over drumsticks. Wrap 1 bacon slice around each drumstick. Secure with wooden picks.

Heat 1 tsp (5 mL) oil in a cast iron frying pan on cooking grid approximately 3 inches (7.5 cm) above coals. Place 6 drumsticks in frying pan and cook for about 10 minutes before flipping. Cook for another 8 to 10 minutes, until internal temperature reaches 170°F (77°C). Repeat with remaining oil and drumsticks. Remove and discard wooden picks. Makes 12 drumsticks.

Cast iron frying pans need to be "seasoned" from time to time. To season your pan, heat it up on the stovetop until its smoking hot, then rub a little oil into it and let it cool. Never put away your pan wet after you've washed it.

Outdoor Chicken with Vegetables

Cooking over an open fire can be a wonderful, rewarding experience provided you keep your fire under control. You want a small cooking fire, not a blazing inferno. If you do not have an established fire pit at your site, you can build one with the help of a small shovel and some rocks. Dig a 2 to 3 foot (60 to 90 cm) hole about 6 inches (15 cm) deep and space out small boulders, about 8 to 12 inches (20 to 30 cm) in diameter, around the perimeter of the hole. The pit will ensure your fire doesn't spread, and the rocks will also serve as a solid base for your cooking grid. Keep in mind that sparks and flying embers are dangerous, so never build an outdoor fire on a windy day.

Boneless, skinless chicken breasts	6	6
Red potatoes, quartered	6	6
Baby carrots	1/2 lb.	454 g
Medium onions, sliced	2	2
Can of corn (12 oz., 341 g)	1	1
Medium green peppers, sliced	2	2
Golden Italian dressing	2 cups	500 mL

Prepare campfire. Tear off 2 pieces of foil about 12 × 14 inches (30 × 36 cm) each and spray with non-stick cooking spray. Divide all ingredients between foil sheets and fold to seal. Place packets on grid over campfire or on a bed of hot coals. Cook for 35 to 40 minutes per side until potatoes are tender and chicken is no longer pink. Makes 6 servings.

Black Bean Chili

Everyone loves a good chili especially when enjoyed in the great outdoors where campfire cooking and chili go together like Simon and Garfunkel. Pair this dish with a fresh French baguette or homemade loaf of sour dough bread.

Cooking oil	2 tsp.	10 mL
Lean ground chicken	1 lb.	454 g
Chopped onion	1 1/2 cups	375 mL
Chopped celery	1/2 cup	125 mL
Chili powder	1 tbsp.	15 mL
Dried oregano	2 tsp.	10 mL
Garlic clove, minced	1	1
Can of stewed tomatoes (14 oz., 398 mL)	1	1
Chopped red pepper	1 1/2 cups	375 mL
Kernel corn	1 cup	250 mL
Can of tomato sauce (7 1/2 oz., 213 mL)	1	1
Hot pepper sauce	1/2 tsp.	2 mL
Can of black beans (19 oz., 540 mL), rinsed and drained	1	1
Sliced green onion	1/4 cup	60 mL
Grated sharp Cheddar cheese	1/2 cup	125 mL
Chopped fresh cilantro or parsley (optional)	2 tbsp.	30 mL

Prepare campfire. Heat oil in Dutch oven over hot coals. Add chicken and cook for about 5 minutes.

Add onion and celery and cook for about 10 minutes, stirring often, until onion is softened.

Add next 3 ingredients and cook, stirring, for about 1 minute, until fragrant.

Stir in next 5 ingredients and bring to a boil. Cook, covered, for 15 to 20 minutes to blend flavours.

Stir in beans and green onion, and cook for another 15 minutes until heated through.

Sprinkle with cheese and cilantro. Makes about 7 cups (1.75 mL).

Dutch Oven Chicken Pot Pie

Because there are so many fabulous recipes one can create with a Dutch oven, we like to keep our old yellow Copco Dutchie close by at all times. Sure, the bottom has become blackened over the years, but the enamel-coated cooking area inside is as pristine today as the day we bought it. The only drawback to Dutch ovens, in my opinion, is their size and weight. They are rather heavy, but the options they present while travelling and cooking in the outdoors are limitless.

Cooking oil	1/4 cup	60 mL
Cans of chicken breast meat	2	2
(12 oz., 341 g, each)		
Minced garlic	2 tsp.	10 mL
Medium potatoes, diced	4	4
Medium onion	1	1
Medium red pepper, chopped	1	1
Milk	3/4 cup	175 mL
Flour	1/4 cup	60 mL
Cans of condensed cream of mushroom soup	2	2
(10 oz., 284 mL, each)		
Poultry seasoning	2 tsp.	10 mL
Onion salt	1 tsp.	5 mL
Can of peas (15 oz., 425 mL)	1	1
Tube refrigerated crescent rolls	1	1
(8 oz., 226 g)		

Prepare campfire. Heat oil in a Dutch oven on a grid placed about 2 inches (5 mL) above open coals. Add chicken and garlic and cook for about 5 minutes.

Add potato, onion and red pepper and cook for about 10 minutes, stirring constantly.

In a small cup, mix milk and flour. Add milk mixture and next 4 ingredients to Dutch oven. Stir and bring to a boil.

Unroll crescent rolls and create a dough layer on top of chicken mix. Cover pot and place on coals to bake. Pot pie is ready when top is golden brown and flaky.

Grilled Chicken Quesadillas

Of all the campfire meals I serve my crew while we're away camping, this recipe is the all-time family fave, especially with my daughters! It is as easy to prepare and cook on the campfire as it is to eat. If you are a big Tex-Mex food enthusiast, this one will rank at the top of your list as well!

Canned black beans, rinsed and drained	1 cup	250 mL
Cooked, chopped chicken	1 cup	250 mL
Kernel corn	1/2 cup	125 mL
Chopped green onion	1/4 cup	60 mL
Jar of roasted red peppers (12 oz., 340 g), drained and chopped	1	1
Finely chopped pickled banana peppers	2 tbsp.	30 mL
Grated Mexican cheese blend	2 cups	500 mL
Flour tortillas (9 inch, 23 cm, diameter)	4	4

Stir first 6 ingredients in a medium bowl.

Sprinkle 1/4 cup (60 mL) cheese in half of each tortilla. Sprinkle about 1/2 cup (125 mL) of bean mixture over cheese. Sprinkle with remaining cheese. Fold tortilla over filling and press down lightly. Spray both sides with cooking spray. Place quesadillas in a large cast iron skillet positioned over, but not directly on top of coals. Brown quesadillas in pan for 3 to 5 minutes per side. Makes 4 quesadillas.

∼ To poke a wood fire is more solid enjoyment than almost anything else in the world.
—Charles Dudley Warner

Chili Panko Trout

Fresh-caught trout are, in my opinion, one of the best-tasting wild fish in all of North America. They are highly prized by sports fishermen, offer superb table fare and are perhaps the most aesthetically pleasing of all finned creatures. If you don't have panko bread crumbs, you can use cornmeal instead.

All-purpose flour	1/3 cup	75 mL
Panko bread crumbs	1/3 cup	75 mL
Chili powder	1 tbsp.	15 mL
Salt	1 tsp.	5 mL
Trout fillets (about 4 oz., 113 g, each)	6	6

Combine first 4 ingredients in a medium shallow dish.

Press both sides of fillets into panko mixture until coated. Discard any remaining panko mixture. Spray both sides of fillets with cooking spray. Cook on greased grill for about 2 minutes per side until fish flakes easily with a fork. Makes 6 servings.

〰 Panko is the Japanese cuisine's version of the bread crumb and is generally used for coating fried foods in Asian cooking. Unlike North American bread crumbs, panko tends to be flaky-looking. Because it is coarser than the North American bread crumbs, it makes a perfectly crunchy crust. Panko comes in two forms, white and tan. White panko is made from crustless bread, whereas tan panko contains all parts of the bread. If it's unavailable at your local grocer's, you should be able to find it at an Asian market.

If people concentrated on the really important things in life, there'd be a shortage of fishing poles.
—Doug Larson

Grilled Salmon with Dill

Salmon makes an ideal meal choice for nutrition and health reasons because it was recently discovered to have some of the highest levels of omega-3 fatty acids—an enzyme that helps reduce the risk of cardiovascular anomalies. Although salmon is considered one of the world's healthiest foods, keep in mind that smoking salmon has been found to substantially reduce its omega-3 content. Wild salmon contains only 3000 milligrams of omega-3s for a 6 ounce (170 g) serving, compared with farmed salmon's 4500 milligrams. It has been noted, however, that farmed salmon may exhibit higher levels of toxic PCBs.

Mayonnaise	1/4 cup	60 mL
Plain yogurt	1 tbsp.	15 mL
Mustard seeds	2 tsp.	10 mL
Ground cumin	1 1/2 tsp.	7 mL
Chopped fresh dill	1/2 cup	125 mL
Salt	3/4 tsp.	4 mL
Lemon juice	1 tbsp.	15 mL
Salmon steaks	6	6

Prepare campfire with a thick bed of coals and place grid about 2 inches (5 cm) above coals. Combine first 7 ingredients in a large bowl. Spread mixture over salmon steaks, making sure to cover meat completely. Grill salmon for 7 to 8 minutes, turning once, until salmon meat separates easily from bone. Serve hot. Makes 6 servings.

Dill has been a household staple for years—since 400 BCE, some historians suggest. And although we know and love dill as a food additive, it seems our ancestors had other uses for it, as well. Dill seeds were burned in the home as an all-natural air freshener. Dill tea was given to people who had trouble sleeping, and medicinally it was used to settle all sorts of tummy troubles. It was also believed to ward off the "evil eye" and repel witches.

Blackened Perch Fillets

Don't let their meagre size fool you: coldwater perch are some of the sweetest, best-tasting fish you will find anywhere. In regions of Canada with an active winter ice-fishing season and solid number of fish, such as Ontario's Lake Simcoe, perch are targeted with regularity. Although perch can be somewhat labour-intensive to clean and prepare, you will be greatly rewarded once they hit the table. Perch meat is firm-textured, low in fat and explodes with flavour when it hits the palate.

Paprika	2 tbsp.	30 mL
Garlic powder	1 tsp.	5 mL
Cayenne pepper	1/2 tsp.	2 mL
Pepper	1/2 tsp.	2 mL
Dried thyme	1/2 tsp.	2 mL
Dried oregano	1/2 tsp.	2 mL
Perch (8 to 10 fillets)	1 lb.	454 g
Melted butter	2 tbsp.	30 mL

Cook your campfire down until you have a nice glowing bed of hot coals. Mix paprika, garlic powder, cayenne pepper, pepper, thyme and oregano in a small bowl. Coat fillets completely in mixture. Place fish in a hot skillet sprayed with cooking spray, and pour melted butter over top. Position skillet directly on top of hot coals and cook until almost charred, then flip over and cook other side. Serve piping hot! Makes 4 servings.

FISH: an animal that grows the fastest between the time it's caught and the time the fisherman describes it to his friends.
—Unknown

Cajun Shrimp "Outback" Foil Packets

Whether you're enjoying a casual weekend at the cottage or trailer or doing some hardcore backpacking, foil pack recipes are a smart and logical choice for campfire use. Aluminum foil is a great and convenient outdoor cooking medium that can often replace the need for a pot, skillet or Dutch oven.

Uncooked extra-large shrimp (peeled and deveined)	1 lb.	454 g
Andouille sausage, sliced	1 lb.	454 g
Cooked corncobs, quartered	2	2
Small red potatoes, halved	1 lb.	454 g
Vegetable oil	2 tbsp.	30 mL
Cajun seasoning	1 tbsp.	15 mL
Chopped fresh parsley	2 tbsp.	30 mL
Lemon, cut into 8 wedges	1	1

Spray 4 sheets of aluminum foil (each 12 inches, 30 cm, long) with cooking spray. Divide shrimp, sausage, corn and potatoes into 4 equal portions and place in centre of each foil sheet in a single layer. Fold up all 4 sides of foil, drizzle with vegetable oil and sprinkle with Cajun seasoning. Fold sides of foil over mixture, covering everything completely, and seal packets closed.

Place foil packets on grill and cook until cooked through, approximately 15 minutes. Unfold packets carefully, sprinkle with parsley, squeeze lemon overtop and enjoy! Makes 4 servings.

Have you ever asked yourself which side of the aluminium foil goes up and which side should touch the food? According to Reynolds Consumer Products, it makes no difference. The shiny and dull sides of foil insulate and conduct heat at the same rate.

One-pot Seafood Paella

The Moors of Spain were the first to invent what is today known as paella. They began cultivating rice around the 10th century, and it became customary to add vegetables, beans and sometimes fish. Later popularized by the Valencians, seafood paella is still widely enjoyed today, even among the avid outdoor enthusiast.

Chicken broth	4 cups	1 L
Olive oil	1 tbsp.	15 mL
Butter	1 tbsp.	15 mL
Onion, chopped	1	1
Garlic clove, minced	1	1
Celery ribs, sliced	2	2
Chorizo or spicy sausage (6 inch, 15 cm, long)	1	1
Medium red pepper, chopped	1	1
Turmeric	1 tsp.	5 mL
Paprika	1/4 tsp.	1 mL
Long grain rice	1 1/2 cups	375 mL
Salt	1/2 tsp.	2 mL
Pepper	1/2 tsp.	2 mL
Peas (optional)	1 cup	250 mL
Packaged seafood mix	2 cups	500 mL

Heat broth in a medium pot.

Heat oil and butter in a cast iron or other deep frying pan about 2 inches (5 cm) from campfire coals. Add onion, garlic and celery and sauté for a few minutes until onion is softened.

Add chorizo and red pepper and fry for a few minutes until chorizo releases its oils and flavour.

Add turmeric, paprika and rice and stir until rice is well coated. Add hot broth, stir well to combine, and bring to a boil. Add salt and pepper. Raise skillet to 4 inches (10 cm) above coals to reduce heat to a gentle simmer and cook, covered, for 15 minutes, stirring occasionally. Be sure to keep covered so it builds up a good steam.

Stir in peas and cook, covered, for another 5 minutes.

Stir in seafood mix and cook, covered, until seafood and rice is cooked to desired tenderness and liquid is absorbed, approximately 20 to 25 minutes. Serve immediately. Makes 4 servings.

Build Your Own Breadbox Reflector Oven

A reflector oven is an efficient way to harness the full potential of a campfire for cooking purposes. With a reflector oven, the heat from even a small fire can be channelled to cook a host of different outdoor meals with ease.

Several homemade reflector oven design options exist, but the simplest and most effective, in my opinion, is an old tin breadbox that has had the front door (or top, depending on the style) removed. Detach the hinged door from the front of the breadbox and place the box on its side with the opening facing you. Halfway up the box, screw in two small support arms on each side, directly across from each other. You can use screw eyes or picture holders, or even 1.5 inch (3.8 cm) screw nails. These support arms will hold the weight of a baking pan, cookie sheet or cooking grid in much the same way as the walls of a conventional oven do.

Place your reflector oven directly beside your campfire so that radiant heat can enter and circulate around the inside of the oven. The aluminum/metal sides of the breadbox will reflect heat in and around your food, cooking it from all sides. There is a bit of a learning curve involved in knowing how long to cook each recipe, so check your food often.

These handy campfire ovens can be used to cook a wide variety of dishes, from shepherd's pie and lasagna to baked good such as cakes and cookies. If you do not have an old tin breadbox, any large piece of aluminum or tin can be folded into the same shape with similar results.

Cheesy Campfire Lasagna

You can easily customize this recipe to suit your taste. Try replacing the ricotta cheese for cottage cheese, or include some spinach or pepperoni slices for a bit of added zip. The choice is yours! Be sure to pair this yummy lasagna with our Cheesy Pull Apart Garlic Bread (p. 36) for a hearty campfire combo.

Olive oil	2 tbsp.	30 mL
Pasta sauce	1/2 cup	125 mL
Lasagna noodles (oven ready)	12	12
Pasta sauce	2 cups	500 mL
Ricotta cheese	1 1/2 cups	375 mL
Grated mozzarella cheese	1 1/2 cups	375 mL
Dried oregano	1 tbsp.	15 mL

If cooking over a campfire, get your coals ready. You'll need a glowing bed approximately 2 inches (5 cm) thick. Coat the inside of a 10 inch (25 cm) Dutch oven with oil to help prevent sticking. Spread first amount of pasta sauce evenly over bottom. Top with 4 lasagna noodles (breaking noodles to fit pot, if necessary), 3/4 cup (175 mL) pasta sauce and 3/4 cup (175 mL) ricotta cheese. Repeat layers. For final layer, use remaining 4 noodles and 1/2 cup (125 mL) sauce and top with mozzarella cheese. Sprinkle oregano over top. Use approximately 1/4 of the coals to create a bed to set your Dutch oven on. Place Dutch oven on top of coals. Cover oven with lid, and place remaining coals on top of lid. Bake for 30 minutes until noodles are tender and cooked through and cheese has melted. Carefully remove Dutch oven from heat. Let stand 5 minutes or so, carefully remove lid, cut into slices and serve. Makes 4 servings.

Grilled Eggplant and Goat Cheese Stacks

Whoever said meat was a requirement of a wonderful meal? This vegetarian grilled eggplant and goat cheese recipe is a terrific, savoury change of pace and a nice touch of refinement for your next campfire outing. When choosing eggplant for cooking, I always look for the smaller ones because they tend to be sweeter with less seeds and have thinner skin, which allows them to cook faster over a campfire. Serve these stacks with thick slices of grilled Italian bread.

Small eggplant, cut into 8 slices (1/4 inch, 6 mm, thick)	1	1
Olive oil	1 1/2 tbsp.	22 mL
Roma (plum) tomatoes, cut into thirds lengthwise	4	4
Olive oil	2 tsp.	10 mL
Salt	1/2 tsp.	2 mL
Goat cheese, crumbled (about 2/3 cup, 150 mL)	4 oz.	113 g
Basil pesto	3 tbsp.	45 mL
Sweet (or regular) chili sauce	2 tbsp.	30 mL
Olive oil	2 1/2 tbsp.	37 mL
Balsamic vinegar	1 tbsp.	15 mL

Prepare campfire until good layer of coals is formed. Brush eggplant slices with first amount of olive oil. Place on hot grill over fire and cook slices until brown on bottom, then flip over and cook until second side is brown. Remove from heat.

Brush tomato slices with second amount of olive oil. Sprinkle with salt. Cook on greased grill for 2 to 3 minutes per side until grill marks appear.

Arrange 4 eggplant slices on a platter or plate and top each with 3 tomato slices. Sprinkle with goat cheese, and top with remaining eggplant slices. Set aside.

Combine remaining 4 ingredients in a small bowl and stir until well combined. Drizzle over eggplant stacks. Makes 4 servings.

Grilled Spanish Stuffed Peppers

Cooking stuffed peppers on the campfire could seem intimidating to some if not for the camper's trusty Dutch oven. The enamelled cast-iron construction of these heavy-duty cooking machines is perfectly suited for cooking over an open fire.

Large red peppers	4	4
Olive oil	1 tsp.	5 mL
Chopped onion	1 cup	250 mL
Garlic cloves, minced	2	2
Smoked (sweet) paprika	1 tsp.	5 mL
Cayenne pepper	1/8 tsp.	0.5 mL
Salt	1/4 tsp.	1 mL
Can of tomato sauce (7 1/2 oz., 213 mL)	1	1
Can of chickpeas (19 oz., 540 mL), rinsed and drained	1	1
Cooked long-grain brown rice (about 1/2 cup, 125 mL) uncooked	1 1/2 cups	375 mL
Green olives, sliced (optional)	1/2 cup	125 mL
Slivered almonds, toasted	1/2 cup	125 mL
Water	1 cup	250 mL
Fresh dill (optional)	4 tsp.	20 mL
Grated mozzarella cheese	1 cup	250 mL

Cut each pepper in half. Remove seeds and ribs.

Prepare a bed of coals and heat oil in a large cast iron skillet. Place skillet on a cooking grid about 2 inches (5 cm) above coals. Add onion and diced pepper. Cook for about 10 minutes, stirring often, until onion is softened. Add next 4 ingredients. Heat and stir for about 1 minute until fragrant.

Add tomato sauce. Bring to a boil, stirring occasionally. Transfer from skillet to a large bowl.

Stir in next 4 ingredients. Spoon carefully into prepared peppers. Arrange peppers in a Dutch oven. Pour water around peppers, place lid on Dutch oven and put back on coals. Cook for 1 1/2 hours. Sprinkle dill and cheese over peppers and cook for 30 minutes, until peppers have softened and slightly browned and cheese has melted. Makes 4 servings.

Chickpea Hobo Packs

Campfire cooking would not be the same without aluminum foil. There are literally hundreds of uses for aluminum foil when cooking over a campfire, and this hobo pack recipe is just one of them. When shopping for aluminum foil before heading off to do some backpacking or camping, choose your foil wisely: not all aluminum foil is made equally. The cheaper brands tend to be thin and breakable, which makes it more difficult to use around the campfire. I always go with the top name-brand foil as it tends to offer the thickest, hardiest aluminum foil and works best in campfire cooking situations.

Cooked chickpeas	2 cups	500 mL
Medium zucchini, cut into 1/2 inch (12 mm) pieces	1	1
Red pepper, cut into wide strips	1	1
Shallots	2	2
Olive oil	1/4 cup	60 mL
Garlic clove, minced	1	1
Dried oregano	1 tsp.	5 mL
Ground coriander	1 tsp.	5 mL
Dried rosemary, crushed	1 tsp.	5 mL
Feta cheese	1/2 cup	125 mL
Hummus	1/2 cup	125 mL

In a large bowl combine first 4 ingredients and drizzle with olive oil.

Add next 4 ingredients and stir until everything is coated evenly.

Prepare 4 pieces of aluminum foil (about 12 x12 inches, 30 x 30 cm, each). Divide vegetable mixture evenly amongst foil pieces, placing it in centre of foil, and sprinkle with feta cheese. Pinch together all four sides of foil and curl under to seal. Place packets on grill about 3 inches (7.5 cm) above coal bed for medium heat and cook for 15 to 20 minutes. Open carefully, and enjoy with fresh hummus on the side. Makes 4 servings.

Easy Rice and Beans

This is one of the easiest and most nutritious recipes you can cook in an outdoor setting. If I were lost in the woods for one week and had but one recipe at my disposal, I would want it to be this one. Of course I would make sure to have a bottle of hot sauce hidden somewhere as well.

Long-grain white rice	1/2 cup	125 mL
Olive oil	1 tbsp.	15 mL
Ground cumin	1/8 tsp.	0.5 mL
Garlic cloves, minced	2	2
Onion, medium, chopped	1	1
Olive oil	1 tbsp.	15 mL
Vegetable broth	1 cup	250 mL
Can of black beans (19 oz., 540 mL), drained and rinsed	1	1
Can of diced green chilies (4 oz., 113 g)	1	1
Small tomato, diced	1	1
Salt	1/2 tsp.	2 mL

Hot sauce, to taste (optional)

Cook rice according to package directions.

Meanwhile, heat a large skillet on grill over hot coals. Add first amount of olive oil and cumin. Cook, stirring, until fragrant, about 20 seconds.

Add garlic and onion and sauté until onion is translucent and soft.

Add remaining olive oil, broth and black beans. Cook, stirring, for 5 to 7 minutes, cooking off most of liquid and letting beans fry a bit.

Add chillies, tomato and salt, and cook, stirring, for another few minutes. Stir in cooked rice and enjoy. Makes 2 servings as a meal or 4 as a side.

Outdoor Mac and Cheese

I have this recipe as part of the vegetarian section, but mac and cheese is one of those meals that everybody loves, vegetarian or not. It is always a great camping comfort food. This campfire version is extra yummy when enjoyed around a crackling fire.

Elbow macaroni	4 cups	1 L
Butter	6 tbsp.	90 mL
Milk	1 cup	250 mL
Flour	4 tbsp.	60 mL
Salt	1 tsp.	5 mL
Pepper	1/2 tsp.	2 mL
Grated Gruyère cheese	2 cups	500 mL
Grated Cheddar cheese	1 cup	250 mL
Grated Gouda cheese	1 cup	250 mL
Bread crumbs	1 cup	250 mL

Cook macaroni according to package directions using a Dutch oven or pot. Drain well and set aside.

Using same Dutch oven or pot, melt butter over charcoals and whisk in milk. Add flour, one tablespoon at a time, continuously whisking until mixture has thickened and you have a roux. Add salt and pepper.

Combine cheeses in a medium bowl. Remove 1/2 cup (125 mL) cheese mixture and set aside. Slowly add remaining cheese to Dutch oven, stirring constantly, until cheese has melted into roux. Add macaroni and stir to coat with sauce. Cover and cook until heated through, about 5 minutes.

Top with reserved cheese and bread crumbs. Cover and cook for an additional 5 minutes. Serve warm. Makes 4 servings.

To avoid unwanted animals in your campsite, make sure all food is stored well in a latched cooler with a heavy rock on it, or locked inside your vehicle. Always keep food away from your sleeping area.

Tasty Eggplant and Tofu Foil Bundles

This recipe is another great vegetarian option that is as easy to prepare as it is delicious. It comes together quickly at the campsite but could also be made ahead of time and placed in foil packets when you are ready to cook. Serve with rice, salad or another side or your choice.

Firm tofu	20 oz.	570 g
Small eggplant (about 12 oz., 340 g)	1	1
Finely chopped ginger root	2 tbsp.	30 mL
Minced garlic	2 tbsp.	30 mL
Soy sauce	1/4 cup	60 mL
Vegetable oil	1/3 cup	75 mL
Green onions or shallots, chopped	2	2

Cut tofu into 16 pieces. Quarter eggplant lengthwise and cut into pieces. Put tofu and eggplant into a resealable freezer bag and add remaining ingredients. Place in a cooler or refrigerate for at least 1 hour to marinate. Prepare your campfire. To cook, divide mixture between four foil pieces and seal securely. Grill bundles for about 10 minutes, turning once. Check that eggplant is tender when pierced. If not, return to grill for 5 minutes. Makes 4 servings.

It's easier to throw sticks on the campfire than to try to restart it when it goes out.
—Cynthia Lewis

Campfire Loaded Baked Potatoes

If you've never tried a loaded baked potato, do yourself a favour and sample the campfire version first! There is something extra special about this recipe when enjoyed outdoors with family and friends. It is one of the few times when potatoes can serve as both a side and a main course. Be sure to bring along lots of extra sour cream. You'll need it!

Large unpeeled potatoes	4	4
Butter	4 tbsp.	60 mL
Salt	2 tsp.	10 mL
Pepper	1/4 tsp.	60 mL
Green onion, chopped	8 tbsp.	125 mL
Grated Cheddar cheese	1 cup	250 mL
Sour cream	1 cup	250 mL

Wash and cut the potatoes into 1 inch (2.5 cm) pieces. Spray 4 large sheets of foil (about 12 inches, 30 cm, long) with cooking spray. Divide potatoes and butter into four and place 1 portion in centre of each foil sheet. Season with salt and pepper. Wrap foil around potatoes and close each packet tightly. Cook on grill of your campfire until potatoes are tender, approximately 25 minutes, turning packets occasionally to avoid burning.

Remove potatoes from packets, top with onions, Cheddar cheese and sour cream. Makes 4 servings.

Advice from a campfire: bring people together, spark new ideas, kindle strong friendships, radiate warmth, no smoking, be a good storyteller, don't burn out!
—Unknown

Backcountry Corn Fritters

This corn fritter recipe will appeal to the whole family and fits perfectly with the outdoor cooking lifestyle. During summer when sweet corn is in season, I usually cook extra and remove several cups of kernels to freeze and store for this recipe. These fritters are terrific made with canned corn but absolutely amazing when made with fresh corn, especially peaches and cream or sweet yellow corn.

Egg	1	1
Granulated sugar	1 tsp.	5 mL
Salt	1/2 tsp.	2 mL
Butter	1 tbsp.	15 mL
Baking powder	2 tsp.	10 mL
Flour	1 cup	250 mL
Milk	2/3 cup	150 mL
Kernel corn	2 cups	500 mL
Green onion, chopped finely (optional)	2	2
Vegetable oil	3 tbsp.	45 mL

In a large bowl, combine egg, sugar, salt, butter, baking powder, flour and milk, mixing well. Stir in corn.

Prepare campfire. In a large non-stick skillet about 2 or 3 inches over hot coals, heat oil until it has reached point to which you can fry (about 360°F, 180°C). Drop spoonfuls of batter into skillet and flatten with spoon. Cook until one side has browned, about 4 to 6 minutes, then flip fritter and brown the second side. Drain on paper towels before serving. Makes 5 servings.

Pesto Vegetable Medley

A delicious variation on ratatouille that is sure to please. This earthy, colourful mix of grilled veggies makes a perfect side for any grilled meat, or you could serve it with fresh French bread or bannock for a light meal.

Basil pesto	1/4 cup	60 mL
Red wine vinegar	2 tbsp.	30 mL
Salt	1/4 tsp.	1 mL
Pepper	1/4 tsp.	1 mL
Sliced Asian eggplant (with peel) 1/2 inch (12 mm) thick	1 1/2 cups	375 mL
Sliced zucchini (with peel), 1/2 inch (12 mm) thick	1 1/2 cups	375 mL
Chopped red onion, cut in 1 inch, 2.5 cm, pieces	1 cup	250 mL
Chopped red pepper, cut in 1 inch, 2.5 cm, pieces	1 cup	250 mL
Whole fresh white mushrooms	1 cup	250 mL

Combine first 4 ingredients in a large bowl.

Add remaining 5 ingredients and stir until coated. Cut 4 sheets of foil about 14 inches (35 cm) long. Spray 1 side with cooking spray. Spoon equal amounts of eggplant mixture onto each sheet and fold edges over to seal securely. Prepare a fire with a nice bed of coals. Place packets, seam side up, on greased grill about 2 inches (5 cm) above coals, and cook for 15 to 20 minutes until vegetable are tender. Makes 4 packets.

Winter Camping Tips

True outdoor enthusiasts do not pack it all away in late fall when temperatures start to drop. With so many great winter camping options in the country, there's no need to stop venturing afield when snow blankets the landscape. I say get out there and enjoy all that our wonderful natural world has to offer! However, there are a few crucial points to consider when winter camping for the first time. These tips may very well save your life.

With much of the camping world shut down until spring, potential winter camping locales are more limited. Do your homework when choosing a location for your winter camping trip. Bear in mind that many national and provincial campgrounds are closed for the season, and scant few private camping areas offer winter camping options. Camping on Crown land is an alternative where provincial regulations allow, but make sure to visit the camping area prior to heading off with your tent and winter supplies. Winter access to remote areas is often limited to snowmobiles or all-terrain vehicles.

You'll need a reliable heat source other than your trusty wood fire when winter camping. A catalytic heater fuelled by naphtha or propane is a must. A quality tent is also extremely important, and you must choose your camping cot and sleeping bag with care. That light-as-a-feather summer sleeping bag just won't cut it in severe cold weather conditions. Instead, choose an extra thick survival or mountaineering-style sleeping bag, rated to minimum -40°F (-40°C). Sleeping off the ground during cold weather is essential to retain body heat, so add a camping cot to your gear. The most efficient winter cots are constructed of an aluminum frame with a light, breathable fiber or nylon mesh top.

During winter trips, your camping cooler and food storage bins actually insulate food from the icy cold. A typical camping cooler that needs to be filled with ice to keep your food cold during a spring or summer wilderness outing will actually prevent your food supply from freezing solid during a winter trip. Camping during the bitterly cold months of the year does take some resilience and a lot more effort, but for those who enjoy the freedom and challenge of spending more time afield, do not let a little snow on the ground stop you. Camp on, my friends!

Old-fashioned Bannock

Bannock is a kind of flatbread that can be cooked over a campfire by wrapping the dough around a tree branch or frying it in a greased skillet. Some cooks add raisins or berries to flavour the bannock, which has long been popular among First Nations and Inuit peoples as well as outdoorsmen and women throughout Canada. Basic bannock can also be made with boiled potatoes added to the dough and is considered especially tasty when eaten fresh after being cooked in lard.

All-purpose flour	2 cups	500 mL
Baking powder	1 tbsp.	15 mL
Butter	3 tbsp.	45 mL
Salt	1 tsp.	5 mL
Warm water	2/3 cup	150 mL
Cooking oil	1 tbsp.	15 mL

Place flour, baking powder, butter and salt in a large bowl and mix with your hands until dough clumps. Slowly add water and mix until dough softens (you may not use the entire 2/3 cup, 150 mL, water). Let dough rest, covered, for 30 minutes.

Divide dough into quarters and shape each portion into a ball. Flatten into a disk about 1/2 inch (1 cm) thick. Heat frying pan on grill over coals and add oil. Cook bannock on both sides, turning once, until golden brown. Alternatively, you can forgo the frying pan and simply twist the dough around a clean stick and hold it over an open campfire until it is golden and crispy. Makes 4 servings.

Campers' Cornbread

The beauty of the sweet cornbread is that it is a great accompaniment for any meal, and it can be a great snack on its own. Although not as popular here in Canada, our neighbours to the south serve and enjoy cornbread with many meals. This recipe is something that fits perfectly with the campfire cooking lifestyle.

Butter	1 tsp.	5 mL
Package of cornbread muffin mix (8 oz., 225 g)	1	1
Egg, beaten	1	
Milk	1/3 cup	75 mL
Can of creamed corn (8 oz., 227 mL)	1	1
Granulated sugar	1/3 cup	75 mL

Prepare a glowing bed of campfire coals. Lightly grease bottom of your Dutch oven with butter.

Pour muffin mix into a large mixing bowl. Stir in egg and milk, and then add creamed corn and sugar. Mix until smooth. Pour batter into prepared Dutch oven and place lid on top. Place Dutch oven on cooking grid 2 inches (5 cm) from hot coals. Shovel a small number of live coals onto lid. Cook for 20 to 30 minutes, until a knife inserted into centre of cornbread comes out clean. Cut into squares and serve. Makes 4 servings.

Keep close to Nature's heart...and break clear away, once in awhile, and climb a mountain or spend a week in the woods. Wash your spirit clean.
—John Muir

Dutch Oven Cobbler

I must admit that I am not a huge fan of desserts; however, this Dutch Oven Cobbler is simply to die for. And without a thick pie crust, it is fairly low in fat. I am a huge supporter of the Dutch oven for outdoor recipes, so I decided to give this one a try. Because this cobbler requires at least 1 hour of cooking time, I knew my fire needed to be a good one, so I planned accordingly. The coals required to sear a steak are much different than the coals required for most Dutch oven dishes. The real trick is in the timing. You do not want to start this meal too early before your fire is ready, or leave it too late so that your coals peter out. I am proud to say that my first attempt at Dutch Oven Cobbler was received with rave reviews!

Can of fruit cocktail (15 oz., 425 mL), with juice	1	1
Can of sliced peaches (15 oz., 425 mL), with juice	1	1
Can of pineapple chunks (12 oz., 341 mL), with juice	1	1
Ground cinnamon	1/2 tsp.	2 mL
Box of golden (or yellow) cake mix (8 1/4 oz., 517 g)	1	1
Brown sugar	1 cup	250 mL
Butter, cut into pieces	1/2 cup	125 mL

Prepare your campfire. Combine fruit cocktail, peaches, pineapple, all fruit juices and cinnamon in a Dutch oven and stir well. Sprinkle dry golden cake mix over top and sprinkle brown sugar on top of cake mix. Place little pieces of butter on top of brown sugar. Cook, covered, over coals for about 1 hour until top is browned and cake has absorbed fruit juices. Makes 8 servings.

〰 You will need to start off with a good-sized campfire to produce enough coals to sustain at least 1 hour of cooking time.

Canadian Campfire Bread Pudding

Is there any dessert more comforting than bread pudding? This recipe is also a great way to get rid of that day-old bread. You can also use leftover hamburger or hot dog buns or even dinner rolls from the night before. Any bread product will work, and they do a great job.

Butter	1/2 cup	125 mL
Bread slices, diced	6	6
Large eggs	5	5
Can of sweetened condensed milk (14 oz., 398 mL)	1	1
Whole milk	3/4 cup	175 mL
Vanilla extract	1 tsp.	125 mL
Maple syrup	1 cup	250 mL

Warm your Dutch oven or cast iron pot over campfire. Add butter and allow to melt. Add bread pieces and cook until toasted.

Whisk eggs in a separate bowl. Whisk in condensed milk, whole milk and vanilla. Pour mixture over toasted bread pieces in Dutch oven. Place Dutch oven on grill about 2 inches (5 cm) above campfire coals. Cook, covered, for about 20 minutes. To test for doneness, push a knife into centre of pudding; if knife comes out clean, pudding is cooked. If not, cook, covered, in 10 minutes intervals until knife comes out clean and pudding is set. Cut into squares and top with maple syrup. Makes 6 servings.

If you find yourself with wet campfire wood, try splitting the wood to expose the drier inner layers and begin burning it from that side.

Campfire Baked Apples

Despite its simplicity, there is something exciting and intriguing about this recipe, no matter how old you are. I recall back in Cub Scouts, when I was 12 years old, Baked Campfire Apples was the first food we learned how to cook over the open fire, and it is a recipe I still make today with my daughters. For an extra touch of sweetness, you could sprinkle the cooked apple with icing sugar.

Large apple (such as Granny Smith or Cortland)	1	1
Brown sugar	1 tbsp.	15 mL
Ground cinnamon	1/4 tsp.	1 mL

Core your apple using a corer or a knife.

Combine brown sugar and cinnamon in a small bowl or cup. Fill apple's hollow core with brown sugar and cinnamon mixture. Wrap apple in a 12 inch (30 cm) piece of aluminum foil, leaving a little tail for a handle. Place in campfire coals and let cook for 5 or 10 minutes. Remove and unwrap carefully (sugar will be very hot). Makes 1 serving.

Some women want diamonds...others just want a hammock, a campfire and some peace and quiet.
—Unknown

Grilled Pineapple

The word "pineapple" is derived from the Spanish word pina and is named for its prickly shape. This sweet tropical fruit is extremely popular in the Caribbean. It is used in a variety of recipes and forms the basis of the popular Caribbean cocktail, the pina colada. When grilled using this recipe, this wonderfully delectable fruit explodes with flavour and sweetness.

Whole fresh pineapple	1	1
Brown sugar	1 cup	250 mL
Ground cinnamon	2 tsp.	10 mL

Prepare and core your pineapple, cutting fruit into 6 wedges.

Combine brown sugar and cinnamon in a resealable freezer bag. Add pineapple and shake to coat each wedge. Place pineapple on preheated grill over fire (no flames) and cook until heated through, about 5 minutes. Makes 4 servings.